PROPHETS & Prophecy

The Ministry of Prophets in the New Testament Church

WILLIAM EMMONS

PROPHETS & PROPHECY

Printed in the USA

ISBN (Print Edition): 978-0-9961701-0-9

ISBN (Kindle): 978-0-9961701-1-6

ISBN (eBook): 978-0-9961701-2-3

Library of Congress Control Number: 2015935304

Prepared for publication by: www.palmtreeproductions.com

. . . .

To contact the author:

www.pdministry.org

. . . .

ACKNOWLEDGEMENTS

I want to begin this book by giving a brief word of heart-felt thanks to my sweet wife Prophetess Esther Emmons, Apostle Rick Callahan, Dr. Ron Cottle, Apostle Rick Menard, Prophets Steve and Rita Fedele, Prophet Phil Cappuccio and Dr. Lance Wallnau. All of you have been friends in life and encouragers in ministry in various ways. I count myself a very blessed man to know you and have worked with most of you. You have spoken into my life when it was needed and provided true guidance. You are all a treasured gift from the Lord and this book is possible because of your investment in me.

Last of all, I want to thank the people of Life Christian Center Church. We have done life together in the Kingdom for nearly thirty years at this writing, and I count that to be both a privilege and high honor. You have allowed me to travel as a prophet all over the world, and you have carried the load without complaint whenever I have gone. What a treasure each of you are to me. Without you this book would never have been possible. All I can say is "Thank You." You are the best!

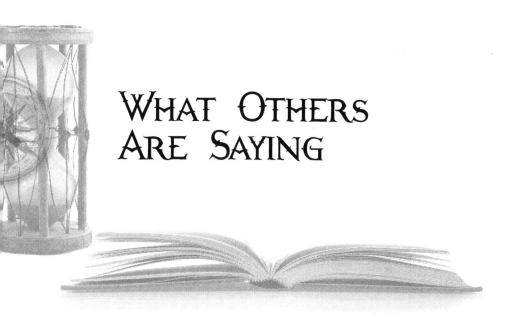

WHAT OTHERS ARE SAYING

"When I opened my copy of this "prophetic handbook" I quickly began to realize that this book was not just light-hearted comments on prophets and prophetic ministry. It was a strong, insightful look at important matters concerning the Bible and the New Testament incidents involving prophets and prophecy. Having known Prophets Bill and Esther Emmons for many years, and having had the opportunity to minister side-by-side with them in prophetic gatherings, I can attest to the authenticity of their ministry, and the accuracy of their prophetic utterances. This book, "Prophets & Prophecy In The New Testament Church" is not theory, but a practical understanding and a tremendous revelation on the topic, with relevancy for the New Testament church today.

Prophet Bill Emmons has taken many years to listen to the Holy Spirit and work through prophetic ministry in his own life. As a result he is now equipped and released to offer these powerful truths to others, helping to build and shape prophetic ministry in their lives. Throughout the pages of this book you will discover insights and wisdom presented by one who has embraced the call to function in the prophetic gifts as God's communicator."

—Apostle Rick Callahan

Founder & President, Maranatha Ministerial Fellowship International
Founder & President, Proceeding Word Ministries International, Inc.

"Prophet Bill Emmons is the real thing! He is an intercessor, a man sensitive to the Spirit of God, and one who loves and respects God's people. These qualities and calling on his life set him apart for God's use as a prophet in the 21st century apostolic reformation.

Prophet Emmons is a spiritual son to Apostle Rick Callahan, my own spiritual son in the Lord, so I know him to be strongly aligned, accountable, and richly equipped for his task.

This book tells Bill's story of his own walk in prophetic ministry. In these pages he drops nugget after nugget of insightful truths that are priceless for those with this special anointing. This book is a practical guide and manual for operating in the prophetic. I recommend it and its author to any church, network or conference seeking the Word of prophecy."

—Ronald E. Cottle, Ph.D., Ed.D

Founder and President Emeritus, Christian Life School of Theology (CLST)
Apostolic Council of Transformational Servant-Leaders (ACTS)

"If you are a five-fold ministry gift to the Body Of Christ, "Prophets & Prophecy In The New Testament Church" should be one of your equipping tools. Whether you are a seasoned veteran, and up-and-coming leader or just getting your feet wet in the things of the Spirit, this is a must read.

For the Apostle, this brings forth clarity and will help you avoid headaches and heartbreak in key relationships. For the Prophet, this is a manual for you at every level of prophetic gifting and calling. For the Evangelist, this will empower you in the prophetic power of evangelism. For the Pastor, this will help you to set order and prophetic protocol in the house. For the Teacher, this has been not only well researched, but also well lived. These principles will teach and establish destiny.

I encourage you to read this book, keep it close to your desk and sow it into the lives of the next generation of prophetic voices."

—Apostle Rick Menard
Founder of Ranger Ministries
Northeast Regional Director,
Maranatha Ministerial Fellowship International

"In *Prophets & Prophecy*, Bill Emmons has masterfully combined key and essential elements, thus producing a necessary reference work and guide for all within the church who desire to learn about, and grow in the Spirit's operation through prophetic ministry. First and foremost there is that primary ingredient of scriptural truth. The scriptures contained within this manual provide a sound and strong foundation regarding the role of prophets and the expression of prophecy in the New Testament Church. Then added to the scriptural insights are those additional and essential ingredients, which involve all those things obtained from the wisdom that my dear friend Bill Emmons has garnered through many years of flowing in what has proven to be a seasoned prophetic ministry.

In addition to being a personal blessing to so many within the Body of Christ over the years, Prophet Bill has multiplied and expanded his ability to help in the equipping process through this publication. In my opinion every believer's library under the "prophets & prophecy" section would be incomplete without including his volume. If you are a leader, then I suggest that you study it and use it to help instruct and equip the Saints in this vital ministry. Remember it is incumbent upon every disciple to know just how to speak a word in due season to him that is weary. The volume you are now holding will help you to do that quite effectively. Prophet Bill, thanks again my friend, for giving us this gift."

—Pastor/Prophet Phil Cappuccio
Kingdom Life Covenant Church
Hershey, PA

"This book is a wonderful review of foundational principles that have been established regarding prophetic ministry. In additional to these principles, Bill's personal experience from years of prophetic ministry make this book an educational and enjoyable read."

—Prophet Stephen V. Fedele,
Founder, Prophetic Voice Ministries International

CONTENTS

. . . .

**Surely the
Lord God does
nothing unless
He reveals His
secret counsel
to His servants,
the prophets.**

Amos 3:7

. . . .

THE BASIC FOUNDATION

Even though I am a prophet, I am also just like any other man on planet earth. I love a good book, or to hunt and fish. I enjoy camping, hiking, shooting my pistols, riding my motorcycle and taking my kayak out on the lake. I enjoy a quiet trout stream or a Bar-B-Q. I love to sit by a fire at night or take a walk on the beach at sunset while holding my wife's hand. I just enjoy the life God has given me, and best of all I have found my place in it.

On the other hand I am also a very spiritual man and always hunger for a deeper, more intimate relationship with God. I love to pray in the Spirit, dig into God's Word, teach, preach and prophesy His word to see His Kingdom manifested here on earth. That being said I have the same struggles as you, but I have learned how to get victory over them so they don't rule my life. The point is, even though I am a prophet, I am still human, and so is every prophet you will ever meet. We are simply everyday people who love God, love to speak His Word, and reveal His heart to His Church, but we are still flawed in many ways.

I say the above for a good reason. When the word "prophet" is spoken, many different concepts can come to mind. Some see a wild-eyed desert wanderer with a long gray beard, who leans on a rugged staff and wears rough clothing. Others envision one who comes down off the mountain with the glory of God on them as they spout scripture and convict people with a penetrating look. Yet another version is of ego-centric leaders who say they have special "insight" with God, and use it to manipulate the innocent and financially take advantage of the unsuspecting.

Unfortunately, we have all seen examples of the above, and for the most part they have been exposed and gone the way of the dinosaur. That being said, the truth that has gone unnoticed about genuine prophets is quite simple, elegant and yet profound. It is my desire to lay things out in this book so that you will really understand God's heart when it comes to prophets and prophetic ministry. Ultimately, I want you to be able to separate truth from fiction, and fear based teaching from ignorance and misinformation. If you come away from this writing with that foundation, than my mission will have been accomplished and this book has served its purpose.

What you are about to read is a very candid, honest look at my life as a prophet. It will openly unveil the things I learned over many years of prophetic ministry and the mistakes I made. You will discover who prophets are, how they operate in the New Testament church, and why they are so desperately needed today. My hope is that you may glean from my experiences, both the good and the bad, and be better prepared to walk as a prophetic person in these rapidly changing ends times.

Early Encounters

Much has been said in books and certain circles of the church about the restoration of what is commonly called the "five-fold" ministry. This term comes from Ephesians 4:11-12 where the five foundational ministries of the church are clearly identified as being the Apostle, Prophet, Evangelist, Pastor and Teacher. Ephesians goes on to say that Jesus Himself gave these gift ministries to the church when He ascended on high. Thus they are also called the "ascension gift" ministries and He gave them to perfect His Bride, and bring Her to full maturity.

Most churches today embrace some, but not all, of these five ministries in varying degrees. Of the five, in my experience, the office of the prophet has been the most controversial and least received. Fear, wrong teaching and bad examples have all but driven the heartiest of souls away from embracing this much-needed biblical ministry. I was fortunate enough to be brought up in a local body of believers that taught and tried to embrace all of what Jesus gave to His church. However, even with that good foundation, there was still a great deal of mystery and misinformation surrounding prophets and their ministry, though I didn't know it at the time.

What I did know was that I was called as a prophet from the evening I got saved, on July 11th, 1976. I had a divine visitation and literally walked right into the Glory of God. I was caught up into heaven in His hand and saw and heard things I had never imagined were possible. At that moment I had no idea what prophets were, and my calling was not confirmed until a year or so later. That evening I got a very simple prophetic word from a visiting musical group called "The Bridge." They said, "To sing and to play, the voice of a prophet."

The office of the prophet, and the ministry of prophetic presbytery with the laying on of hands had been restored to the church several decades before my conversion. Yet very few people in the northeastern United States understood the prophetic realm, the ministry of the prophet or the many styles of prophetic ministry that are evident. Fewer still knew how to mentor anyone who was actually called to function as a New

Testament prophet. All of this presented some difficulties for me that were not easily overcome.

Dear friends of mine, prophets Steve and Rita Fedele, lived about 40 miles from me, and they had also been called as international prophets at the same time. They had the good fortune of being part of a much larger church and were mentored by some of the pioneers of prophetic ministry. People like Mickey Mingo, Dr. Eldon Wilson and Rev. Reg Lazell took an interest in them and nurtured the prophetic calling that was clearly on their lives.

I unfortunately, had no one to take me under their wing and teach me the principles of balanced prophetic ministry.

> **I had no one to take me under their wing and teach me.**

As a result I spent my early years floundering along, making mistakes and striving for opportunities, in hopes that my ministry could find a valid place of expression. Eventually Mickey Mingo further confirmed my calling to prophetic ministry, and the Fedele's also recognized this calling on my life and that made a huge difference.

In the early 1990s I began doing a yearly prophetic conference in my own church and then God arranged it so Steve Fedele and I began traveling together several months a year doing prophetic presbytery across New England. This became a "school of the Spirit" for me and it revolutionized my life and ministry as a prophet in many ways. Through it I found the training, instruction, correction and mentoring I desperately needed to become more seasoned and balanced as a prophet.

Since those early years I have learned a great deal. I have much greater understanding and experience as a prophet, and I have discovered the different aspects of the ministry prophets can bring. This has come through God-ordained connections, spiritual revelation, soaking in His presence, solid teaching and personal correction from many mighty men and women of God. Over time, I have had the privilege of watching, listening to and working alongside some of the most respected prophets and apostles alive today. Each impacted and changed me in ways that were very needful for what God called me to do.

All these things helped to produce not only the kind of ministry I have, but more importantly, the kind of minister I am. As you read over this work be sure to keep this as your primary focus. Never forget that God's first desire is to fully develop you. Only then will He have what He needs to fully develop your ministry. If you can keep this focus as you grow in the Lord, you will be blessed and so will all who hear you. Without this important reality being in place, you and the ministry God gave you, will be an easy target for all the deception this world has to offer.

The Prophetic Realm

Understanding the prophetic realm, and how it is established in the economy of God, is essential for all believers who want to live as a "prophetic" people. As one grows in this area of understanding, much of what God is doing in the earth today will become clear. Thinking prophetically is foreign to many Christians, but it is not foreign to God. 2 Chronicles 20:20 says:

> *"And they rose early in the morning and went out to the wilderness of Tekoa; and when they went out, Jehoshaphat stood and said, "Listen to me, O Judah and inhabitants of Jerusalem, put your trust in the LORD your God, and you will be established. Put your trust in His prophets and succeed."*

In addition Amos 3:7 adds the following:

> *"Surely the Lord GOD does nothing unless He reveals*
> *His secret counsel to His servants the prophets."*

The main thrust here is that God uses prophets and their ministry to build His people and His church, especially in times of trouble. A case in point is found in Ezra 5. The captivity of the Jews is in full force, yet they have favor with King Darius to rebuild the walls of Jerusalem, and the house of God. At this very time opposition begins to rise up, but right in the middle of it we see the prophets playing a key role in moving the work forward. Here we read:

> *"When the prophets, Haggai the prophet and Zechariah the son*
> *of Iddo, prophesied to the Jews who were in Judah and Jerusalem,*
> *in the name of the God of Israel, who was over them, then*
> *Zerubbabel the son of Shealtiel and Jeshua the son of Jozadak*
> *arose and began to rebuild the house of God which is in Jerusalem;*
> *and the prophets of God were with them supporting them."*
>
> EZRA 5:1-2 NASB

The Hebrew word for "supporting" used in this text, means to establish, uphold, strengthen, build up and refresh. It was the prophetic word, and the support those words brought, that encouraged and refreshed the people so the work would continue. In fact, this is always the effect of genuine prophetic ministry, and true prophetic words. Simply put, God uses both to help His people become established and fully succeed.

God uses prophets to build His people. Beyond this, Amos 3:7 says God uses the prophet to reveal His secret counsel when it is needed. The Hebrew word for "counsel" is "sod" which means intimate fellowship and secret plans. That is, God tells them what He is doing and why

He is doing it. This being the case, there can be no doubt that we need solid, mature prophetic ministry more than ever today in the church, and in the marketplace. Just as the Jews met resistance to God's plan when it was time to rebuild and restore things, we also meet resistance as we serve God. It is the ministry of balanced prophets that can support, build, refresh and encourage people to move forward in what they have been called to do.

On a personal note I have experienced firsthand, the benefit my prophetic ministry has brought to businesses. On occasion I have had the honor of businessmen calling me for my insight as a prophet to help them with critical business decisions. At times I felt a check, but other times I had God's "go ahead," and set up a meeting to hear their heart and pray with them. In those instances God gave me wisdom, clear direction and specific insights that prophetically identified problem areas. This in turn maximized their business and brought a substantial financial increase.

As a result of that prophetic word, they financially sowed back into my ministry and that was a great blessing to me. I certainly did not meet with them for the purpose of financial gain. However, that increase was God's way of pouring His finances back to me. In case you missed it, this is how things are supposed to work in God's Kingdom. Financial increase is part of the fruit God's kings harvest in the marketplace. They in turn become a financial supply for those who minister before Him and His Church.

So, those who desire to understand prophets and the prophetic realm, must first embrace what God has established in His Church according to Ephesians 4:11-12. All five ministries mentioned here are needed to perfect the Saints so they can do the work of the ministry. To ignore or reject even one of these ministries reveals a limited understanding of Scripture, and rejects what God intended. Without accepting and embracing all five ministries, little progress will be made since part of the ministry needed to move things forward is missing. If He gave all five, then we need all five, and it's just that simple!

In addition, there must also be an understanding of four important key ideas:

1. the kinds of prophets which exist;

2. the various levels of prophecy which operate;

3. the different types of prophetic meetings and how they function;

4. the kinds of prophecy that exist.

These four essentials are the foundations of the prophetic realm and it's important to keep them in mind. The basic concepts just mentioned can unlock the destiny of all who understand them. For this reason, and others we will yet discuss, the ministry of seasoned prophets is vitally necessary to bring the church into full maturity.

Prophets And Their Sphere Of Authority

Even a brief review of Scripture identifies the fact that several different kinds of prophets actually exist. Some are called to function specifically within their local assembly, while others have ministries that extend out to a given city or region. Some prophets minister to entire nations, while there are those who operate on an international or global level. The Greek word "metron" is used in Scripture to identify the specific measure of authority any prophet has. What authority is exercised, and the full sphere of that authority, is based upon the metron the prophet is called to.

The metron one has is very important when it comes to prophetic ministry, or for anyone called to five-fold ministry. It literally speaks of the actual reach, or the size of the grasp, or territory that someone has in the spirit, and in the natural. This word is used by the apostle Paul in 2 Cor. 10:13 where he says:

> *"But we will not boast of things without our measure ("metron"),*
> *but according to the measure ("metron") of the rule which God has*
> *distributed to us, a measure ("metron") to reach even unto you."*

This essential truth must be clearly understood by every prophet if they are to be effective and successful in their ministry. They must know the specific place of their calling, the actual reach of their ministry and the sphere of authority and influence God has granted them. Their metron is the only place they will be fully anointed to function and really begin to flourish.

Luke 2:36-37 clearly identifies Anna in her specific metron of authority. In this case it is found in her local synagogue. It says;

> *"And there was a prophetess, Anna the daughter of Phanuel,*
> *of the tribe of Asher. She was advanced in years, having lived*
> *with a husband seven years after her marriage, and then*
> *as a widow to the age of eighty-four. And she never left the*
> *temple, serving night and day with fastings and prayers."*

Anna's calling was to that specific assembly and she gladly functioned in her place, waiting to release the ministry God had given her. As a result of her obedience, she had the enormous privilege of revealing the Christ Child when He arrived on the scene. Had she been dissatisfied with what appeared to be a limited sphere of ministry, she could have easily stepped beyond her place of anointing and missed the very thing God created her to fulfill. However, because she fully embraced where she was called to be, she was a clear prophetic voice that identified the things of God to her generation when they happened.

Today, many who feel the "call" to ministry immediately have visions of sugarplums dancing in their head. They see themselves in a worldwide, international, televised crusade, where tens of thousands of people crowd around them because they are the man or woman of power. It is this self-seeking, egocentric, pride-filled concept of ministry that has gutted the local church. This false, worldly idea of ministry has been the downfall of many just because they expected it to be something God never intended. Unfortunately, the Bride has been the one who has really paid the price.

Perhaps this is one of my biggest concerns for those who head out and are gone for a few years of training at high profile, mega training centers. Please don't misunderstand what I just said. These are wonderful places to be set on fire, and receive instruction and training in Kingdom principles from world-class ministers. People will most certainly hear and be touched by those they would never encounter in their local church. These places instill a concept of ministry that releases people from the confines of the church walls and into the streets, and that is so desperately needed.

Being trained in a global atmosphere does not necessarily translate into ministry on a global scale.

Unfortunately, those trained in this global atmosphere may also assume their own ministry is on a global scale. They often see themselves doing conferences, guest appearances and special meetings from church to church. While a few are actually called to this level of ministry, the vast majority of people are called by God to serve in their local church. However, this idea typically cuts across the grain of what they have experience, and now desire to do. We had an example of this happen in our own congregation not long ago.

One of our most promising, fired up young ladies was sent off with our blessing and encouragement for a few years of training. She received amazing teaching, met global ministers and even spent time in Mozambique (among other places) ministering with IRIS ministries. When it was time to return home and pour back what she had learned into this place, her vision was no longer for the local church. She was convinced she had a more global level of ministry and was destined to release the power of God to multitudes. However, her ministry was not yet clearly identified, nor was she fully spiritually defined, and this proved to present conflicting visions.

She is a wonderful spiritual daughter of ours, but upon returning home she was very unsatisfied and felt restrained after all the global adventure. She was convinced her call would remain unfulfilled unless she got out of the area. So, she moved back to Tennessee believing God would open ministry for her there. When nothing happened she moved to Atlanta hoping to find her spiritual breakthrough in that place, but still nothing happened. She was without clear church connections and without clear direction for her life all this time. Finally another move came, and eventually she landed back here somewhat disheartened, confused and depressed.

At this writing we are greatly encouraged because she has plugged back into our local church. She has started using and developing what God placed in her to fire up this place, and we are so glad. Now that this young lady is connected back into the church, she is finding ways to pour out the treasure God placed in her. She has an open door for the ministry she's been seeking, and our local church is getting the benefit. The point being made is very simple. We have to love His Bride more than the ministry He gave us to perfect Her. When we are ministry driven, and not Bride oriented, we have missed God's heart, and that will always pose a huge problem.

How is it that things like this can happen? Well, to begin with those with a desire for ministry often hold in low regard the idea of "only being in the local church." This, though few will admit it, is considered of lesser value, somewhat insulting and beneath their high calling. As a result, there have been very few Anna's left to reveal Jesus when He has come to a local congregation. Ministers can be so hungry for "ministry" that they often forget where they were called to minister. In the end, they also neglect whom they were actually called to serve. This means that the Bride of Christ has been considered unworthy of our very best. She has been abandoned by the very one's God gave to love, protect and perfect Her so She will be ready for Her returning King.

Keeping this in mind, you must also remember that the scope of any prophet's ministry is only limited by the boundaries God has placed upon it. Once this is clearly understood, every prophet is free to function and develop within those boundaries to the maximum extent they can. Within their own metron there are no limits, and every prophet should continually grow and develop, hoping to expand and enlarge what God has given into their charge.

Thus, some prophets may be called by the Lord to function in a local church, as was Anna. Others may be released to move in an entire city, and their measure of authority would extend to all the people in that place. We see an example of this in the prophet Jonah. Jonah 1:1-2 reads:

> *"The word of the LORD came to Jonah the son of Amittai*
> *saying, "Arise, go to Nineveh the great city, and cry against*
> *it, for their wickedness has come up before Me.""*

Jonah may have functioned in other areas as well, but it is clear that his primary calling in this season of life was to the specific city of Nineveh. God may choose to reassign a prophet to another church, region or nation, but once an assignment has been given, that is where the prophet and their ministry must be faithful to stay. Why is that? That's because you don't get another assignment until you faithfully complete the one you have!

If you remember the situation with Jonah he eventually made it to Nineveh and did prophesy God's word to the people. However, he was not so pleased with God's mercy on them, and sat down waiting to see if judgment would come. What we discover is that in the end God's judgment came to him instead. It's interesting to note that he was not released from his assignment until not only the city repented, but just as important, his heart was set in right order as well. Perhaps there is a lesson we all need to learn in this!

In Scripture, many prophets had a regional calling and a regional measure of authority.

In Scripture we see that other prophets had a regional calling, and their measure of authority was exercised within a specific area of the country. Agabus seems to be one of these since he is identified as being connected with the regions around Judea, Jerusalem and Antioch. Acts 21:10 and Acts 11:27-28 says this about him:

> *"And as we were staying there for some days, a certain prophet named Agabus came down from Judea."*

> *"Now at this time some prophets came down from Jerusalem to Antioch. And one of them named Agabus stood up and began to indicate by the Spirit that there would certainly be a great famine all over the world and this took place in the reign of Claudius."*

We see from Scripture that there are other prophets, such as Zephaniah and Moses, who are called to a national level of ministry. They have authority to speak into the lives of entire nations or people groups, and to national leaders. In Zephaniah 2:5 and Exodus 3:10 we read the following:

"Woe to the inhabitants of the seacoast, The nation
of the Cherethites! The word of the LORD is against
you, O Canaan, land of the Philistines; And I will
destroy you, So that there will be no inhabitant."
"Therefore, come now, and I will send you to Pharaoh, so that
you may bring My people, the sons of Israel, out of Egypt."

What kind of prophet one is called to be, and how great their sphere of authority is, is determined by God alone. Thus, some prophets are called to the nations of the world. Their ministry is global in reach and they move under a mandate from God to every people group under heaven. Jeremiah is an example of a prophet with this global metron of authority. In Jeremiah 1:10 we read:

"See, I have appointed you this day over the nations and
over the kingdoms, To pluck up and to break down, To
destroy and to overthrow, To build and to plant."

It is interesting to note that metron not only has the concept of identifying the measure, scope and boundary of influence under a person's control, it also has the idea of a specific, limited portion. Thus, even though 2 John 3:34 says that God gives the Spirit without measure (metron), He also limits where that metron can operate. Prophets who ignore this biblical truth can quickly end up outside their sphere of authority and be in deep trouble.

I want to make sure you got that point. God gives the Spirit without measure to every believer. We are unlimited in the realm of spiritual resources when we serve the living God. We will never run out of what we need to fulfill the plan of God for our life, because He never runs out. However, where that abundance will be poured out is found in a very specific and clearly defined place of service. When we step outside our metron, the flow of provision from that source will simply dry up.

I experienced an interesting example of this over the years. I began to learn about prophetic ministry on a local level but I knew my call was much more. However, every attempt I made to move beyond where God was training me at the moment ended up in a mess. I got discouraged, became frustrated and felt rejected because doors I was forcing open kept slamming shut. Yet, once I was functioning properly in a local setting, I was then thrust into prophetic presbytery and began to travel regionally and internationally into Canada. As I pressed into that calling, God eventually opened a global door for me to be on the apostolic board of Maranatha Ministerial Fellowship International.

With MMFI, my metron became world-wide. At the same time I was also given a huge amount of favor in Quebec, Canada and Albany, the capital of New York State. The predominant church in Albany has multiple campuses, and I had prophesied these into existence over the course of several years. The leaders of this church embraced my wife and I as personal friends and recognized us as seasoned prophets. They have highly valued us before their congregations, and recognized us before the city's spiritual leaders. This was nothing I planned, but it was God's plan for me because I was willing to grow with the metron He gave me.

So, it is plain to see that personal desire, ability, gifting and driving ambition have no bearing on what God has set in place for each prophet. However, driving ambition and gifting do have the potential to cause a great deal of trouble within a prophet's ministry. These things all have the capacity to push the individual way beyond what God actually anointed them to do. That, my friends, is a very dangerous and frustrating place to be.

The Bible indicates that anyone stepping beyond their sphere of authority will most certainly have problems. The fact is, those who push beyond their actual metron will

Stepping beyond your sphere of authority causes God's favor to lift from you.

not have God's Spirit or favor upon them as they go about trying to fulfill their ministry. This is a revelation that many need today, and it makes Isaiah 61:1 come alive with new meaning. Here we read:

> *"The Spirit of the Lord GOD is upon me,* **because** *the LORD has anointed me to bring good news to the afflicted; He has sent me to bind up the brokenhearted, to proclaim liberty to captives, and freedom to prisoners …" (Emphasis added.)*

In looking at this Scripture, take special notice of the word "because." Any time you see this word, it means there is an action/reaction event going on. One thing happens *"because"* something else happened first. In this instance the Holy Spirit is upon, and flowing through the person, *"because"* the Lord anointed them to do something specific. That means what you are anointed to do will always have the power, favor and authority of the Holy Spirit backing it up. When you step beyond your metron of authority, the Spirit of the Lord will not be upon you, or anointing you, in that activity.

Thus Isaiah and Jesus both could boldly say; *"The Spirit of the Lord is upon me because He has anointed me to …"* They knew that walking in what God anointed them to do would bring to bear the power of His Spirit upon them to accomplish that specific assignment. The anointing and favor of God are placed upon you when you are called to a specific task. That's because God always empowers and anoints people to do the thing He created them to do.

This simple but profound truth is the key that unlocks and releases all true, Spirit led ministry. Once you know what you are anointed for, all you need to do is get in that place and the Holy Spirit will be upon you to get the job done. Step outside your place of anointing and in that moment the favor of God, and the power of God will be gone. Anything you accomplish at this point is by human effort, and you are now operating by natural ability. This also means you have become an easy target for demonic infiltration into all of your actions.

Make sure you just got what I said. The devil is happy to anoint you for the wrong thing, even if you do it for the right reason. He knows that such naturally based human effort will ultimately end up taking you in the wrong direction. So, even if you can get good results through natural effort it will ultimately steal, kill and destroy what you were really called to do. This is exactly why it is so important to patiently wait on God and find out what He has called you to do.

James 3:13-15 tells us that it takes wisdom from God to know if our works and conduct are really motivated by the Lord or by our own self interest. If God is in it, His wisdom is the guiding light and we are blessed. However, when we operate from a natural place of strength and motivation then James classifies all of it as *"earthly, sensual, demonic."* In this day and age it is important to know the difference if we are going to have true and lasting fruit

A Practical Example

This principle applies in the market place as much as it does for those called to minister specifically in the church. I know a man who has looked for a break through most of his life in the area of finances. He has received several prophetic words about being a conduit for money, and he always has a heart to give. However, the financial flow God intended him to have just never seemed to manifest.

The woman he married is well educated and works in the public sector. Her organizational skills, ability to do research and love of detail have brought her several promotions. In addition she was an art major in college and her knowledge of art has been a great blessing in their antique business. Over time they have both developed quite an eye for appreciating and recognizing the value of all types of artistic expression.

One day at a garage sale they asked if there might be any paintings available and discovered there was one piece. Out came something from a back room that made their hearts jump. It was an old oil-on-board of a woman washing clothes. The owner explained it had belonged to his parents and they had brought it with them from Europe after World War II.

After some discussion they purchased the piece, and when they got home, something wonderful happened. By doing research they found it was indeed from Europe and it was called "The Laundress." A few months later it was sold at auction in Boston for many times what they had paid for it. Since that time this kind of thing has been repeated again and again. The point is, this is their real metron, the place of their strong anointing, and it is here that their financial blessing and spiritual influence is always very clear in their lives.

> **Operating within your sphere of authority brings God's favor.**

Both of these people have pastoral hearts, and a clear gift to teach, but these were never fully defined within our church. You must understand that a teaching "gift" is very different from those called to be five-fold teachers. With the gift of teaching, individuals take the revelations of others and break them down so they can be clearly understood. This means the gift operates with ease in organizing and explaining information, and giving the application of biblical principles.

However, anyone called as a five-fold teacher receives fresh revelation, and that is very different. A five-fold teacher consistently releases deep insights and new understandings that set people on fire. They unfold burning truths that impact the heart in ways that were never understood before. It's very common to have that "Ahaaa!" moment when you are listening to a five-fold teacher. That's when the proverbial light bulb comes on in your heart and your spirit begins to jump up and down with excitement because you just ate "Manna" that came straight from heaven.

My point is, this couple had a gift to teach and had a definite calling in the area of support and encouragement to the church leadership. They said themselves that they were called to lift up the hands of the elders and felt comfortable in that role of support. Through our lack of understanding we mistakenly assumed their desires, gifts and talents would qualify them as five-fold ministers on our eldership team. As a result they were invited to be in that position a few years earlier and we soon discovered this was the wrong decision.

This is a great couple who really loves God, and they supported our church in many ways for years. Yet after conflict and misunderstandings with the eldership team they ended up stepping down in great frustration. The end result was bad all the way around mainly because they were wounded and felt as if they had been personally rejected. We could never get things resolved and after struggling for some time, this wonderful couple finally backed out of everything and eventually left the church.

God's heart is for each of us to find our metron and stay there. When we don't, it causes all kinds of problems. People get hurt, the church suffers and everyone misses out on the blessing those gifts should have been. What did we learn? If God is using you in wonderful ways in one area, don't automatically assume this means you can move into something else. God's Word does say that *"a man's gift makes room for him."* However, only choosing to walk in God's calling is what brings us into the high place of our anointing. If you can get this concept embedded in your heart, it will prevent you from a lot of disappointment and confusion in your life.

Every person, especially those who are called to any level of five-fold ministry, must get this concept clearly fixed within. The place of anointing is where the real metron of influence is found. This is why it is so important to find your place of anointing and stay there. The apostle Paul clearly said this in 2 Cor. 10:13-16. He stated that people should never step beyond their measure. They should stay within the sphere of authority God has apportioned to them, because that is the high place of His blessing.

Every prophet must know their actual sphere or metron of authority, as well as the literal place of ministry they are called. If they want the Spirit of the Lord upon them, and flowing through them, they must know who they are, what they are anointed to do, and where they are anointed to do it. Once this is clear they can function in that specific realm with great ease and amazing authority. If they move outside their place of anointing, the Spirit of the Lord will not be upon them, and confusion will always result.

Once a prophet is in the wrong place, or doing the wrong thing, the enemy has a field day. He knows that they will soon discredit themselves, become frustrated, and may even be disqualified from the ministry they really do have. Over the years I have found this to be the single biggest element that destroys the credibility and real potential of those called to be genuine prophets of God. Stepping into the wrong place with the right gift, is a sure set up for failure.

When someone has a clear calling to prophetic ministry, they will often begin walking in it with great enthusiasm. In time however, they wrongly assume their success is evidence of much greater things. Unhealthy ambition, poor character development, emotional instability, no submission to authority and pride will all bring them to the place of what I call "terminal misconception." This is the natural belief that success and anointing in one area automatically qualifies us for bigger and better things. The problem is, what we currently have might be the bigger and better thing God had for us. However, when we refuse to see it, because we want something else, we step beyond the place of our ministry, and that is a disaster in the making.

When terminal misconception is left unchecked, it will push people far beyond what God actually called them to do. Once this happens, the anointing on them lifts and one bad experience soon blends into another. The ministry and minister in this condition will quickly become clouded, and this sets them up for numerous problems. This in turn opens the door for personal offense, uncertainty, a spirit of criticism and finally doubt. In that environment the ministry is sure to collapse and the minster will eventually give up. Then "another one bites the dust," as the old song goes, and this becomes the sad reality for many who really are called as prophets.

I have seen this deadly combination destroy the most promising ministry in a few short years. The best way to avoid such a tragic scenario is to stay in prayer and stay under authority. Once you have found your specific metron, those in authority can release you into it. In addition, remain teachable and be properly trained by more seasoned prophets. Only through this kind of personal relationship can prophetic ministry, and the prophet themselves, remain pure and balanced. Without it, the enemy can blow about even the best of us until we, and our ministry, are both shipwrecked.

The sphere of
authority God has
given you is the
highest place of His
blessing on you.

PROPHETS AND THEIR DEVELOPMENT

Basic Kinds Of Prophets

In my frame of reference, there are two basic kinds of prophets mentioned in Scripture. Other prophets may disagree with me on this simplification, and that's fine. However, after all the years of prophetic ministry I have done, and all the prophets I personally know or minister with, this is how I feel the Lord broke things down for me. In addition, insight from James Goll's book "The Seer" helped to clarify part of this concept as well.

One group of prophets we find in Scripture are those which I call "word" prophets. The other group falls under a category called the "seer" prophet. There is a third group that seems to be evident, where they operate from both realms and flow in either direction. I call these "blended" prophets. We will, for simplicity, focus our attention on the first two groups and only make brief mention of the last.

The thing that makes such a strong distinction between prophetic styles is found in how the particular prophet manifests their ministry. This determines what their ministry nature is, and how these things cause that ministry to actually be released. The great diversity in prophetic expression is based upon two specific things. Number one, it relates to what the actual nature of the prophet is. Secondly, it relates to the way in which the prophet gets their revelation from God. These things make the "word" prophet and the "seer" prophet very different. Their personal nature, how they deliver their message, and how they get it in the first place are the keys to that difference.

One major distinction between the two is that the seer functions from a deeply relational and intimately personal place with the Lord. A genuine seer views their primary ministry as being a relational revelation of God's heart to His people. They often spend a great deal of time waiting and soaking in God's presence. It is from this place of soaking and waiting that they touch God's heart and find their full prophetic expression. Their clearest, and most accurate revelations always come through this process of waiting, seeking and soaking.

In 1 Samuel 9:9 the writer tells us that in old times the word "seer," which is the Hebrew word "ra-ah," was often used. Eventually "ra-ah" was replaced by the Hebrew word "nabiy" or "nabi," which is translated in English as "prophet." I mention this because understanding these Hebrew words gives great insight into the different prophetic natures and expressions prophets can have. These words actually relate more to *how* each kind of prophet gets their revelation from the Lord, than *what* they do once they get it.

In the original language, the word "seer" meant, to behold, to stare at, to discern, to experience and gaze upon intently. It also had the concept of looking at, looking upon, or to be near in order to perceive. In addition it could mean to view or see visions. With this in mind, it is clear that the prophet, who is a seer, predominantly gets what they get by waiting, gazing upon, beholding God and just being in His presence.

This is why a seer hungers to get near Him, soak in His Glory and understand the things of the Spirit from that relational perspective. Experiencing His presence is the key to life and revelation for every seer. It is the spiritual fountainhead of their prophetic call. You will find seers in a place of gazing upon the Lord until they know they are filled with His heart. From that vantage point of personal intimacy, their prophetic ministry finds the God-ordained flow and full expression it was intended to have.

A seer's prophetic ministry finds the God-ordained flow from the vantage point of personal intimacy.

In Ps 27:4 David, who was a seer, makes a profound statement that brings clarity to this point. His source of ministry comes out as we read;

"One thing have I desired of the LORD, that will I seek (pursue, search out, inquire, beg) after; that I may dwell (abide, inhabit, remain, sit, live in the sense of being married to, settle in, stay and wait peacefully and with great satisfaction) in the house of the LORD all the days of my life, to behold (gaze on intently, envision and look at with open eyes) the beauty (delightfulness, favor, glory and majesty) of the LORD, and to enquire (wait upon and meditate) in his temple."
(Expanded translation used to add emphasis.)

The word "behold" in the above Scripture is the Hebrew word "chazah." The NASB Greek-Hebrew Dictionary, and Strong's Greek and Hebrew Dictionary say that this word means, "to gaze upon, to perceive and mentally contemplate with pleasure, to specifically have a vision of, or a prophetic revelation of someone or something because of personal experience." Knowing this makes it easy to understand why seers do what they do, in order to get what they get. They saturate themselves in His Presence and then flow in their ministry from that place of deep, relational intimacy.

My wife Esther is a seer in every sense of the word. What she desires most in life is to get before God every chance she can, and just wait there for hours. She loves to do this and can worship and soak in His presence for days on end. Until she understood her calling to this, approaching ministry any other way brought her great frustration. She produced less fruit and often went away from times of prophetic ministry irritated and empty. However, as we both came to understand the seer's lifestyle, everything changed. Her level of ministry, and the impact it had on people, all went to a new place. She felt great satisfaction and the pleasure of God, rather than frustration in trying to function in a way contrary to how God made her.

Prophets who are not seers, on the other hand, tend to operate from a very different perspective. A "word" prophet functions with ease from a place of raw, proactive faith. They see their ministry as being primarily one that acts as a mouthpiece for God. They are just as passionate about revealing the mind and heart of the Lord, but they typically are not as relational about it. This is because they can do what they do without the kind of waiting and soaking that causes a seer to flourish.

I am more of a word prophet, and word prophets are action oriented. They see themselves like the voice, hands and feet of God. Unlike the seer, a word prophet often has to learn how to release the knowledge of God with the heart of God. This is a major difference and it is a major problem for those of us with this kind of prophetic ministry. Word prophets really have to work on getting God's heart. This is because their prophetic ministry can spring them into action at a moment's notice, from His head or thoughts. They have the capacity to get a "download" of God's thoughts in the Spirit, and can run with them before they ever feel His heart in the matter.

The word prophet must still have soaking times to build their personal relationship with the Lord. However, it is not necessarily viewed as being required preparation for operating in their gift mix. Their prophetic calling and natural makeup blend in such a way that they often operate boldly, and more proactively, rather than emerging from a place of soaking in His presence. This is a major issue that has to be fully grasped in order to see the danger it presents to those who receive such ministry. The above is very important to understand, and we will go over it in greater detail later in this book.

Acts 11:28 and Acts 21:10 identify a prophet by the name of Agabus who is a "word" prophet. In both instances he arrives on the scene and boldly obeys the Lord by speaking and acting out exactly what the Lord told him to do. No seeking, no soaking, no gazing or time caught up in God's presence. He came in the Spirit with the mind of God, and just released what needed to be said and done. This kind of bold, unhesitating action is the hallmark of a "word" prophet.

As for the blended prophet, there are many clear examples of them in scripture. These people seem to operate in both realms. At times they may function like a seer and spend a season gazing upon God. At other times they will walk boldly into a situation and just fire off the word of the Lord. Isaiah and Ezekiel are among those who fall into this group. If you examine their ministry you will see them flowing both ways, depending on the need of the moment.

Perhaps I should state that I am more of a "blended" prophet since I do operate out of both realms. In reality, 75% of the time, my flow is that of a "word" prophet, but occasionally God calls me to function the other way. I have to admit, I find it much easier to move from the place of raw, proactive faith, but the internal heart change God works in me in those seasons of seeking and soaking have impacted me deeply. In fact, because of this I have gained a much deeper appreciation for the ministry of the seer, and I better understand why their style of ministry is so vital to the Church.

Both seer prophets and word prophets have their strengths, and weaknesses. This is the exact reason why both are needed in the Body of Christ. Together, along with the blended prophet, they provide a wonderful balance that gives us insight and clarity into God's prophetic nature. It is amazing to see how God uses different people with different prophetic styles to reveal the fullness of His heart. This is why it's so important for every prophet to value what another prophet brings, and learn to enjoy and honor them in the way they bring it.

All prophets must seek the heart of God. It can't be stated strongly enough that every prophet must seek God, study His Word, pray in the spirit and worship the Lord on a deep and regular basis. Without these essentials, their ministry will be shallow and lack the power and clarity the Lord intended. In fact, these are essentials in the life of every believer, if they plan to move beyond basic Christianity. These things are spiritual keys that unlock us all. Only through them can we fulfill our destiny and run the race in a way that brings pleasure to the Lord and satisfaction to us.

The Place Of Prophets

It needs to be said at this point that people should never exalt prophets, or any other member of the five-fold ministry. No one is ever to be treated with favoritism, because this is not God's way. However, five-fold ministers do need to be honored according to what God has done in their lives.

This is one reason why you will never hear me calling a pastor by their first name in public. I will say "Pastor Frank," Evangelist Bonnie" or

"Prophet Jones." I may call them by a first name in private if they have told me to do so, but I will never say Frank or Bonnie publically. I do this because I want to respect them before others for what God has anointed them to do. The world will provide plenty of dishonor, but Romans 12:10 says, *"give preference to one another in honor."* We need to set a good example and give honor to God's servants every chance we get.

Matthew 10:41 says; *"He who receives a prophet in the name of a prophet shall receive a prophet's reward."* When we honor and receive a prophet as a minister of God, we set ourselves up to be a candidate for reaping all the rewards the prophet brings with them. Until the church learns how important it is to honor each other, including prophets, it will continue to miss the great reward and rich treasure that is within each.

We must all understand that God has no favorites. Job 34:19 says that God *"... shows no partiality to princes, Nor regards the rich above the poor, For they all are the work of His hands...."* In fact 1 Cor. 12:11 goes on to say; *"But one and the same Spirit works all these things, distributing to each one individually just as He wills."* In other words, it is God's decision alone to manifest a gift, or set someone in the Body of Christ as a prophet. It will never be the result of personal desire, hard work or ambition. Because of this, no prophet has the right to brag on anything they do, It is simply Christ in them, the hope of glory.

The prophet, who is emotionally and spiritually mature, will also be secure in their specific level of prophetic ministry. They won't build themselves up, crave recognition, compare their ministry to that of another or desire to be exalted in any way. In spite of the fact that many Christian's have the tendency to do all of the above to prophets, when it comes to motivation, mature prophets will never encourage such behavior.

The seasoned prophets I know, and have worked with, don't want special treatment, and desire nothing more than to hear

God's voice clearly so they can bless His people. They seek to do what God says, when He says, and do it with a pure heart. Once you find a man or woman of God who operates this way, make note of them and realize you have found a storehouse of God's treasure. If you honor and listen to such people, and do what they say, the rewards they bring will bless your life in many wonderful ways.

How Prophets Operate

I am frequently asked, "How do prophets operate?" or, "Exactly how do prophets hear from God?" The answer to this question is very simple. Every prophet is nothing more than a spiritual radio or television. They have a God-given capacity to tune in and receive broadcasts from the Spirit realm. They also have a mandate from God to speak what they receive, when they are told to speak it. How they deliver that message is really the only thing that remains under the control of any prophet, and that is a key issue yet to be explained.

As a prophet uses the spiritual apparatus God gave them, they become aware of what is going on in the realm of the Spirit. They may hear, see, think, feel, taste or smell what is happening in the invisible world. They don't make things up from their own imagination, and they don't decide who this revelation is to be given to. God reveals what He wants to His prophets, and then tells them who it is for, and when it is to be delivered. As a result, those who receive ministry from a genuine prophet should never get upset with what is said, even if they have an issue with how it may have been delivered.

A good example of this is found in 2 Chronicles 16:7-10. As you read the Scriptures below keep in mind that the prophet was simply delivering a message. However, take special note of how King Asa behaved toward the messenger. His reaction reveals something very important, and that is the condition of his heart!

> *"At that time Hanani the seer came to Asa king of Judah and said to him, "Because you have relied on the king of Aram and have not relied on the LORD your God, therefore the army of the king of Aram has escaped out of your hand. "Were not the Ethiopians and the Lubim an immense army with very many chariots and horsemen? Yet, because you relied on the LORD, He delivered them into your hand. "For the eyes of the LORD move to and fro throughout the earth that He may strongly support those whose heart is completely His. You have acted foolishly in this. Indeed, from now on you will surely have wars." Then Asa was angry with the seer and put him in prison, for he was enraged at him for this ..."*

What King Asa did is like getting mad at your television and smashing it because of what has been said on the evening news. Such behavior certainly does not change the truth that has been revealed. However, how you react to the message, most certainly does impact your ability to benefit from it. The response someone has to a prophetic word is nothing more than a true reflection of their own heart condition.

Your response to a prophetic word impacts your ability to benefit from it.

A bad reaction to a prophetic word exposes the very thing God may have been trying to address in the first place. As a result, when anyone gets angry with a prophet for a genuine prophetic word, they are really getting angry with God. It is much better to first examine any prophecy you don't like in the light of Scripture, and then check your own response to it. If you have to, make all the necessary attitude adjustments first so that you can really benefit from what has been spoken.

Another example of this is found in 2 Chronicles 18. Here the king of Israel is about to go out to war after forming an alliance with King Jehoshaphat. Before they leave, Jehoshaphat wants a word from the Lord so Ahab consults his 400 false prophets. However, all of them speak to him under the influence of an enticing spirit (2 Chron. 18:19-21). Even though they are all in agreement, Jehoshaphat still wants to hear from one he knows to be a genuine prophet of God. He says the following in verses 6 through 8:

> *"But Jehoshaphat said, 'Is there not yet a prophet of the LORD here that we may inquire of him?' And the king of Israel said to Jehoshaphat, 'There is yet one man by whom we may inquire of the LORD, but I hate him, for he never prophesies good concerning me but always evil. He is Micaiah, son of Imla.' But Jehoshaphat said, 'Let not the king say so.' Then the king of Israel called an officer and said, 'Bring quickly Micaiah, Imla's son.'"*

Note how Ahab responded to God's prophet. He hated the man and had him locked in prison simply because he did not like the message he brought. The condition of Ahab's heart is revealed by how he responded to what was said. Notice also that Ahab's servant tried to instruct Micaiah on what to speak in order to keep the peace. However, he demonstrates the tenacity every genuine prophet must have when confronted with adversity. Here we read:

> *"Then the messenger who went to summon Micaiah spoke to him saying, 'Behold, the words of the prophets are uniformly favorable to the king. So please let your word be like one of them and speak favorably.' But Micaiah said, 'As the LORD lives, what my God says, that I will speak.'"*
> —2 CHR. 18:12-13 NASB

In the face of great danger, and under pressure due to what others had already spoken, Micaiah shows just what he is made of. He begins by giving the king exactly what he wants, as a way of saying he would submit under the king's authority. Yet, when pressed to really speak what God was saying, he releases the truth and his words were not well received. As you read the passage below from 2 Chr. 18:16-27 (NASB), note how the heart condition of each person is revealed when the word of the Lord is spoken.

> "So he said, 'I saw all Israel Scattered on the mountains, like sheep which have no shepherd; And the LORD said, 'These have no master. Let each of them return to his house in peace.'"

> "Then the king of Israel said to Jehoshaphat, 'Did I not tell you that he would not prophesy good concerning me, but evil?'

> "And Micaiah said, 'Therefore, hear the word of the LORD. I saw the LORD sitting on His throne, and all the host of heaven standing on His right and on His left.'

> "And the LORD said, 'Who will entice Ahab king of Israel to go up and fall at Ramoth-gilead?' And one said this while another said that.

> "Then a spirit came forward and stood before the LORD and said, 'I will entice him.' And the LORD said to him, 'How?'

> "And he said, 'I will go and be a deceiving spirit in the mouth of all his prophets.' Then He said, 'You are to entice him and prevail also. Go and do so.'

> "Now therefore, behold, the LORD has put a deceiving spirit in the mouth of these your prophets; for the LORD has proclaimed disaster against you."

> *Then Zedekiah the son of Chenaanah came near and*
> *struck Micaiah on the cheek and said, "How did the*
> *Spirit of the LORD pass from me to speak to you?"*
>
> *And Micaiah said, "Behold, you shall see on that day,*
> *when you enter an inner room to hide yourself."*
>
> *Then the king of Israel said, "Take Micaiah and return him*
> *to Amon the governor of the city, and to Joash the king's son;*
> *and say, 'Thus says the king, "Put this man in prison, and feed*
> *him sparingly with bread and water until I return safely."'"*
>
> *And Micaiah said, "If you indeed return safely,*
> *the LORD has not spoken by me."*

In the end, Micaiah's words proved true, and the battle they entered into was a disaster for both kings. Micaiah was vindicated when his word came to pass, but the sad thing is, the disaster could have been avoided had they believed what the prophet said. Those in authority only had to open their hearts, receive instruction and honor the messenger. Had they done this, they would have been spared the death and destruction that came upon them.

In the book I wrote entitled *Unlocking Prophetic Presbytery* I go into much greater detail about other important issues that profoundly affect the ministry of the prophet. Such things as character development, submission to spiritual authority and developing a proper style of delivery are all addressed. We encourage the reader to get a copy of this book if they desire more information on these important areas.

Prophets As Time Travelers

Not long ago God showed me that as a prophet, I am actually a time traveler. That is because I have the ability to come and stand beside the Lord in order to view the life of others from His perspective, which is outside of time. That may seem like a strange concept but it is true. In order to speak into the past, address the present or release the future to an individual, I will often view or experience those events I am going to prophecy about. The only way that can happen is if God allows me to be there with Him at those times. In other words, God and I are both "present to the moment."

Remember, He views everything from an eternal "now" perspective and can see the beginning and the end of our lives as a single unit of time. He is present to the moment in every event of every life, in every age. That is possible because He invented time and then placed us in it as finite beings. When Adam and Eve fell, time became a relevant, restraining factor for all mankind on the earth. Thus, when God says He is the "Alpha and the Omega, the Beginning and the End," He is not giving us a revelation about Himself. He is giving us a revelation about who He is to us. How can He say, "I am the beginning and the end" when He is the eternal God who has no beginning and has no end? Quite obviously those references are for our benefit not His!

Let's look at it this way. Imagine your life as a line on the ground that you can see in front of you. You can easily see where it starts and where it ends. If you are young it will be short and if you are old it will be much longer. Imagine that everything on earth has it's own time line as well. Some will be long, say 1000 inches, and could represent the time of the Roman Empire. Others will be short, perhaps 3 inches and represent the 80 or so years of a human life. In fact some might be just a dot since they represent the life of a butterfly or perhaps that of a child that was aborted in the womb.

God is the only One who can stand back from all these time lines and actually look at them from beginning to end in the same instant. That is possible simply because He is outside of time, and we are living in it. From this outside perspective He can view both the beginning and the end of every life with ease. Thus, He sees your beginning and your end, but not as a past, present and future event. For God, your life is a single event and any moment of it can be viewed whenever He wants. This is why I say He is "present to the moment." He is present in every moment of every life because He is outside all of the constraining time limitations. The point is, since the fall, every created thing but angels are bound by these God-ordained limits of time.

As a prophet, I get to stand with God outside of time on a regular basis. I am allowed see the time line of people's lives from His perspective in heavenly places. He allows me to look at the life and events of those He wants me to prophesy over. In a moment of time I get a snapshot, glimpse or image of events from that person's time line. Some are from their past, some are from their present and some may be from their future. I see them as God sees them, and for me these events are all "present to the moment" as well. I can see them with the clarity of something I am experiencing right now, and that is what I prophesy.

> **Prophets have the privilege to see the time line of people's lives from God's perspective.**

When I operate as a prophet I am simply speaking what I am seeing, hearing or feeling in that present moment. What's hard to grasp is that it may actually have happened 40 years in the past, be happening now or it might not happen for another 25 years in the future for the one I am speaking over. But for me, as I speak, I am actually experiencing what I am saying as if it is happening at that moment. The fact is, for me it is happening at that moment and that's why I can speak it with such clarity. This is why I say that a genuine prophet is outside of time, and "present to the moment" with God, when they are prophesying.

A Personal Example

About the year 2003 I was in Newport, Vermont doing prophetic presbytery with two other prophets at Life In Christ Fellowship. When I laid my hands on the pastors I was immediately caught up in the Spirit and found myself standing in a large, multi-story brick building with high ceilings. I saw that the facility was located on top of a hill and that it had lots of small windows that faced out over a lake. I said that it looked like it was a factory or a store, and that it would actually be the place God was going to relocate the church.

You have to understand that I was not just speaking this as a prophetic word. I was actually in the Spirit with God, viewing everything outside of time. I could feel the wood floor, and smell the brick and mortar. I was literally looking out through the wall of small windows and seeing the lake sparkling below me. I was hearing the hollow sound of the empty rooms and seeing the high white ceilings. God allowed me to stand in this building, in the future, and I was simply describing to the pastors what I was experiencing at that very moment.

Eleven years after I spoke that prophetic word, my wife and I were back in Newport, Vermont ministering at Life In Christ Fellowship. When I stepped up to preach I realized I was actually standing in this exact building, and it was the fulfillment of that prophetic word. When I mentioned that fact to Pastors Allan and Janet Bishop who were sitting in the front row, they smiled and said to the church, "it doesn't get any more accurate than that!"

Just for the record let me explain that the new church facility is a multi-story brick building, located on top of a hill. It has many small windows that overlook Lake Memphremagog in Newport, Vermont. You can see the sunlight sparkle off the surface of the lake from the sanctuary. This facility was once a factory that was converted into a store that is now home to this growing, vibrant church. All I can say is God is good and His Word never, ever fails!

The Nonlinear Nature Of God

Let me go one step further and point out that God does not see time as we do. He does not view time or experience it in a linear fashion. Since He is outside of time He never moves, thinks or embraces any event as if it moves from past, to present, and into the future in a straight line. From His timeless perspective, events are viewed and can be revealed in any order He decides because they are all happening in the "now" of that moment. You have to grasp this basic principle if you are to ever understand the true nature of prophecy from God's point of view.

One experience I had with this touched me deeply. I began to pray for a woman one evening in a meeting and the moment I touched her I went into the Spirit and saw her about 35 years in the past. I found myself standing outside a building and looking through a second story bedroom wall at night. The woman was an eight-year old child at this time, and she was hiding under a bed. I could see her and see right through the floor and down into the driveway. In the driveway there were two police cars with flashing lights and I saw two officers come into her room. They dragged the girl out from under her bed, down the stairs and into the police car. She was terrified and screaming for her mother as they carried her away to a foster home.

What shocked me was that I was there, viewing, feeling and living the experience with her in full color, full sound and full emotions. In that moment I realized God had given me the chance to see and feel what she had been through. I was actually there, present in that moment of her personal history. A second later I found myself back in the church and I was speaking about what God wanted to do in her future. Things concluded as I finally related what had happened to her just two hours before that brought her to the meeting in the first place.

This demonstrates a deeper truth, which is a key that unlocks the flow of every true prophetic word. People must never assume a prophetic word is linear in time when they get it. Nothing in Scripture ever indicates a prophetic word must be locked into a linear time flow. The example found in Genesis 46 is a powerful case in point. Let's take a moment to examine exactly how this worked in the life of Jacob.

In Genesis 46 Jacob is on his way to Egypt to join his son Joseph, and he has an encounter at night with God. The Lord gives him a magnificent prophecy that at first glance seems rather straightforward. Here we read:

> Then God spoke to Israel in the visions of the night, and
> said, "Jacob, Jacob!" And he said, "Here I am." So He said,
> "I am God, the God of your father; do not fear to go down
> to Egypt, for I will make of you a great nation there. I will
> go down with you to Egypt, and I will also surely bring you
> up again; and Joseph will put his hand on your eyes"

What we find in this passage is a very clear example of the non-linear nature that prophecy can have. Unless you notice the word Jacob receives literally jumps back and forth in time, you have missed a major concept in how God actually thinks. Let's take a look and see how this all works from a real time perspective.

We begin with *"I Am God."* This is in the immediate present. Next comes, *"the God of your father,"* which is a reference to the past, as Jacob's father is long dead. Then we read, *"Do not fear to go down to Egypt."* Apparently Jacob was remembering the mess Abraham got into in Egypt when he brought back Hagar and birthed Ishmael. God is addressing his emotional state in the present about past events. Next we read, *"For I will make you a great nation there."* In a few years the Jews will have multiplied in the land of Goshen to become a very large group of people. However, another king would arise who did not know Joseph. The Israelites would continue to enlarge in the land and the new king would begin to oppress them. So, this part of the prophecy is actually speaking of at least one-hundred or more years in the future.

Then we read, *"I will go down with you to Egypt."* This is back to the present and on into the next month for the trip down to Egypt. Now God says, *"and I will also surely bring you up again."* This is literally a reference to 430 years in the future when the whole nation is finally released from Egyptian bondage under the leadership of Moses. Finally we read, *"and Joseph will put his hands on your eyes."* In the final prophetic phrase God speaks about Jacob's death, which is 17 years in the future. This is fulfilled when Jacob dies at age 147, and Joseph literally places his hand on Jacob's eyes to close them.

God stands outside of linear time.

This is just one prophecy, to one man, yet the time line God lays out jumps back and forth over a span of almost 500 years with no indication that it is doing so. Imagine what you would think if you were the recipient of this word. Do you see why people might seem a bit confused at Jacob's death, and perhaps even begin to doubt the prophecy because he was never brought up out of Egypt? Even though Jacob died, it was still a valid word to him in God's non-linear prophetic time. This revelation is quite a shock for most people since we are so locked into a linear frame of reference.

When we realize that time may not be relevant to the prophetic things God speaks, it can be very unsettling in every way. What I mean is that time itself, and how it is marked off in the Spirit, holds some powerful and unexpected implications. Hearing and accepting a prophetic word, does not nearly hold as much importance as understanding the principles of non-linear prophetic time. Until you grasp this biblical principle, your concept of when and how God will do things, will go through constant upheaval.

Consider the prophecies about Jesus and the point will become even clearer. One prophecy said Jesus would be from Nazareth. Another said God would call His Son out of Egypt. Yet another declared He would come from Bethlehem. How could all of these be true? In fact the Jewish leaders argued this very point. However, these prophecies were not spoken in linear time. They actually covered a span of over 33 years. Thus, when we read "in the fullness of time," it always refers to the full unfolding of prophetic events in their own prophetic time. This is usually not the linear flow of time that people are comfortable with, but prophets must learn to live with.

Very few prophets know when and how God intends to fulfill what He has said. Can you wrap your mind around the possibility that part of a valid prophetic word you receive today could actually be in God's heart to be fulfilled by your great, great, great, great, great grandchildren and not by you at all? In other words, it was generational. So, the word you are so upset about because it has not yet come to pass, even though you have waited for more than 15 years, may actually be speaking of an event that is 250 years in your family's future. For Jacob it was a 500-year wait. What makes you think your prophetic word is any different? Could it be in the heart of God to actually fulfill your word long after you are dead and buried? It sure is food for thought … isn't it?

Why is this so important to know? Well, if someone dies before their word is fulfilled it does not necessarily mean the prophet missed it. Nor does it mean that the person did something wrong and prematurely brought their life to an end. This is just human, natural, linear thinking and it is not thinking prophetically. It could be that the prophecy was just spoken into the atmosphere over a person's life to prime things for an event in their family's future generations. So, don't let your faith be shaken, or automatically begin to question the prophet's reliability or the word itself. How does the reality of generational prophecy fit into your current concept of a prophetic word? For most it does not fit at all, yet like it or not, generational prophecy is a very real part of the prophetic equation in God's Kingdom.

You must embrace the truth that prophecy in God's eyes is more often event oriented than it is connected to linear time. Until you do, you will be prone to discouragement, doubt and the deception of the devil, simply because your word has not come to pass as you assumed it would. Unless we understand the non-linear nature of God, and let go of a crippling linear mindset, we will never understand why God does what He does. For anyone called to be a prophet, linear thinking basically becomes a limiting factor that puts a blockage right in the middle of their entire ministry.

> **In God's eyes, prophecy is more event oriented and less about linear time.**

I hate to rock your world but this simple revelation gives a whole new meaning to the Scripture where Isaiah says, *"My ways are not your ways and My thoughts are not your thoughts."* Just the very concept of God's non-linear existence and nature, should be enough to make you rethink all of what you have been taught about basic biblical eschatology. This is why I believe much of the end time teachings we have all accepted as fact on the Book of Revelation will be revisited and reconsidered in the days ahead!

Prophetic Bullseye

What most people have never been told is that when you receive a genuine prophetic word, a prophetic "bullseye" gets painted on you. That is, you become a known target for both heaven and hell to go after. Heaven targets you to bring you into a place of maturity, and hell targets you to destroy the expression of Christ that God wants to manifest through you. Like it or not, you are marked and that means the warfare Paul spoke of in first and second Timothy really begins in earnest.

Why does this happen? It happens because genuine prophecy releases a shock wave into the Spirit realm. Remember, the devil is the opposite of God, but he is not God's equal. He does not know the future, he has no revelation of spiritual things and he is left in the dark about what God is doing. Spiritually he really is blind, deaf and dumb. Most people don't understand this truth and they give the devil way to much credit.

Don't ever forget that he and his demons had no clue who Jesus was at His birth. He didn't know where He would be born, or when, so he had Herod slaughter thousands of male children from new born to the age of two trying to kill the Lord. That means the devil also has no clue who you really are either. You are basically living in a protected, hidden place because demonic powers have this huge blind spot. All of them lack genuine understanding, insight and revelation when it comes to the things of God.

However, once your prophecy is spoken into the atmosphere and you hear it, the church hears it, heaven hears it and demonic forces of hell hear it as well. It actually sends a shock wave into the spiritual environment that makes heaven rejoice and terrifies hell. The enemy learns for the first time that he now has to contend with another expression of Christ on the earth, and that means his forces are being stretched thinner and thinner with each unveiling of ministry.

So, when you get a prophecy, especially one in prophetic presbytery, you have finally been uncovered for all creation to see. The enemy now knows for the first time, who God made you to be, and what you are called to do. The place of hidden obscurity you once enjoyed is now gone. That means you must get ready for the warfare to be ramped up in your life. Why is that so important to know? It's important because the gap between where you are and where God called you to be has a name. It's called "fiery trials"! In other words, strap in and hang on bucko, because the ride to fulfill that word is about to begin with full vigor.

The bigger the gap between where you are, and where you are headed, the more fiery trials you will have to go through in order to get there. In all honesty, every time the Lord gives me a "big word" to speak over someone about their great future ministry, like a calling to the nations, I almost feel sorry for them. That's because I am well aware of what they will have to go through to be made ready for that word to manifest in their life. It is no quick or easy process, and I am sad to say that many don't make it. Why? Because many are not willing to be humbled, and will not make the changes that are necessary. Without the required personal and spiritual transformation, no prophetic word will ever come to pass.

I was doing prophetic presbytery with two other prophets in Canada not long ago, and a young man came to me full of admiration and spiritual passion after our first meeting. He said to me, "I want to do what you do," and he asked me to pray for him toward that end. My response seemed to be a surprise when I said, "Only God can do that, but to do what I do, you will have to go through what I went through. Are you ready for that?"

Let me put it to you in the most simple and straightforward way I can so you don't miss this important point. If Jesus had to die and go through hell in order to fulfill His heavenly call, you are not exempt from the same process. David had to run for his life and live as a fugitive in the desert all those years to be prepared as God's king, and so will you. There are no shortcuts to maturity, and only those willing to train well, and run their full race to the end, will get the prize. Everyone begins well, but I can tell you for a fact that very few end that way. What you end up with is really determined by what you do more than you can possibly imagine.

Being A Target

Think about this for just one moment. Jesus encountered no problems until Herod uncovered the prophecy about His birth. Then He, Mary and Joseph had to flee for their lives into Egypt while all the boys age 2 and under were demonically murdered. David was a happy shepherd until the prophet Samuel came, poured the anointing oil on him and gave him the prophecy of his future as king. Immediately a demon was assigned to King Saul who then became obsessed with murdering David.

Want another example? Joseph had no issues until he got those prophetic dreams and spoke them out to his family. Next thing you know he is on his way to Egypt as a slave and ends up in prison. In each case the prophecy painted them as a target and set heaven and hell in motion to go after them. Heaven wanted to bring them to full maturity while hell's design was to bring them to a premature and fruitless end.

Psalm 105:18-19 says that Joseph was afflicted with fetters and he was laid in irons *"until the time that his word came to pass."* Then it goes on to say *"the word of the Lord tested him."* Until he was ready to walk in the prophetic word, that same word was the agent of testing in his life. Heaven and hell came after him at every level to prepare him for what he was called to do on earth. Until he was fit to manifest the prophecy, the prophecy continued to manifest it's work in him. Understand that this was no quick or easy process, and it will work exactly the same way in your life!

Take special note of the word "test" in this passage. It is the Hebrew word "tsaraph." This same word is used elsewhere in Scripture for the smelting and refining of gold in a blast furnace. It is used in connection with the work of a gold or silver smith as they hammer, shape and prepare precious metal. This is the fiery trial Joseph needed to prepare him to become a vessel of honor and the leader that saved Egypt. It's also the kind of treatment everyone can expect to encounter as God prepares them to manifest the design of God that has been prophesied over them.

> **Refining is a necessary process for every prophet.**

If you still have visions of grandeur floating around in your head about the amazing ministry you will have as a prophet, arm yourself with another vision as well. It's the vision of Daniel in the lion's den, Joseph locked away and forgotten in prison and David being hunted for years by Saul. Think of the offering slaughtered on the brazen altar, and burned before the Lord of Hosts. That's where you are headed first, in order to be made ready for that great calling in your life. Let me ask again, do you still want to be a prophet?

There is a reason why the animals had to be tied to the horns of the altar. They heard the bellowing of the ones that had gone before them and they could smell the freshly spilled blood. They saw the smoke and smelled the acrid scent of burned flesh that filled the air. It was a messy business for the priest and a deadly one for the animal. What's the point? Flesh never dies easily or willingly, and that includes my flesh and yours. It has to be dragged in, tied up and held in place in order to be killed. Are you really ready to embrace that kind of lifestyle to fulfill your calling?

If you fail to get this fixed in your heart and mind, you will end up as one more casualty on the battlefield of ministry. Once those called as prophets get this revelation it tends to knock the shine off the apple, so to speak. Everyone wants the authority, power and recognition of being a recognized prophet, but few want to be chastened by God, the devil and man, so they can walk there with humility and integrity. In speaking these honest truths I am letting you know exactly what is in store for you if you move on. Unless you have this spiritual revelation living inside you, you will not be able to endure the war that is going to be unleashed against you once you say "yes."

The other thing you have to realize is that no prophet can give you what they don't have. In addition, they can't impart to you anything unless God has specifically instructed them to do so. That may shock you but it's absolutely true. No prophet can go around laying hands on and imparting everything people want, just because they want it. There is a good reason for this and we need to really understand and consider why this is so.

First of all, prophets are not God. We can't just pass out gifts like someone handing out presents on Christmas morning. Only God can tell us what to impart to His chosen vessels, and we are called to faithfully do just that. The other thing is that people really don't know what is best for them. Sometimes what they want actually could destroy them if they got it, and God knows that. So, even if we did lay hands on you for what you desire, if it was not in God's plan, nothing but false hope would be imparted.

This is quite dangerous because it means the prophet gave you nothing, but you believe that you got what you asked for. This opens a deadly door for your flesh and your soul to have partial success in false ministry. The enemy is always glad to anoint our self-centered, fleshly, soulish activity when we press for something God never called us to do. We will have initial success, but in time confusion always sets in. This is because you can only go so far under your own natural strength and ability. Without God's anointing, everything you try to do will eventually fall apart.

I have been approached on several occasions by young prophets who were impacted by my ministry. Apparently they were impressed with what I did and were zealous for a ministry like it of their own. They subsequently asked if I would lay my hands on them and impart a double portion of my anointing and my prophetic call. Here is a news flash that might shock you. I want a double portion of what I have. If it were that easy I would lay hands on myself! When God so instructs, I can give you what He says, but I can't give you what I don't possess. That's just how the Kingdom of God works. Let me say with all honesty that it's time for us to get a grip on Biblical reality and become settled in these important spiritual truths.

Let's Pray

> *Jesus, I am willing to go through whatever it takes to fulfill the highest calling in my life. I will not shrink back from the fire that must purge me, or from the water that must wash me. I want to be fully prepared for the fullness of what You called me to be. I know I can do all things through Christ who strengthens me. So Lord, strengthen me for what lies ahead and keep my vision on the prize. I ask this in Jesus name! Amen!*

Now that I have completely messed with your mind, let's move on to the next chapter. In it I will attempt to bring a bit of much needed light to how prophecy is actually manifested. It is set up into different specific levels of authority, and different ways in which it can impact those who receive it. My hope is that by the end you will discover the spiritual implications of how God intends to use each level of prophecy in His Church, and in the marketplace.

THE LEVELS OF PROPHECY

Just as there are different kinds of prophets, with different measures of authority, there are also different levels of prophecy God established in His Kingdom. Each level has its own strength and place of operation. The levels of prophecy are broken into three distinct groups, and each has a different function and a different degree of authority. It is very important to understanding what these are, and how they operate, if you are to really grasp how the prophetic realm functions.

The Three Prophetic Groups
Group 1: God's Word To His Church

This first group contains the two highest levels of prophecy. The first is the prophecy of Scripture, which is "God breathed." This level is infallible, unchangeable and it is the standard by which all other prophecy is judged. The second is made up of the "canonical" prophets. These are the men and women who actually did the speaking forth of Scripture. Through them the Bible we hold today was actually spoken into existence. Please take note that the canonical prophets have been gone for 2000 years. No one speaking since the Apostles is speaking forth Scripture.

Group 2: God's Gifts To His Church

The second group contains levels three, four and five of the prophetic, and they are all God's gifts to the Church. Level three is given by Jesus to equip and mature the church. Level four is given by the Holy Spirit to edify and comfort the church. Level five is given by the Father to make each individual member of the church special and unique.

Group 3: God's Testimony To His Church

The sixth and final level of the prophetic is the Spirit of prophecy. This is God's testimony to His Church. When the Spirit of prophecy is flowing Jesus is testifying about what He is doing in and with His Bride. It also functions in every believer as they share their personal testimony with others. This in turn builds people's faith and releases the power of the Holy Spirit to do mighty things. When the Spirit of prophecy is really flowing, the atmosphere can become so charged that anything is possible.

The chart which follows identifies each of these levels in a visual form and this may help you better understand what was just said.

The Six Levels Of Prophecy

LEVEL 1
PROPHECY OF SCRIPTURE
2 Pet. 1:20
The Written Word of God

LEVEL 2
CANONICAL PROPHETS
Deut. 18:20/Acts 21:10
Spoke the Word that became Scripture

GOD'S WORD TO THE CHURCH

LEVEL 3
THE OFFICE OF THE N.T. PROPHET
Eph. 4:11-13
Given by Jesus to the Church

LEVEL 4
THE GIFT OF PROPHECY
1 Cor. 12:7-11
Given by the Holy Spirit to the Church

LEVEL 5
THE GRACE GIFT OF PROPHECY
Rom. 12:6
Given by the Father to the Church

GOD'S GIFTS TO THE CHURCH

LEVEL 6
THE SPIRIT OF PROPHECY
Rev. 19:10
The Testimony of Jesus to the Church
& Our Personal Testimony

GOD'S TESTIMONY

The Levels Of Prophecy

Most people do not realize that prophecy is not simply a single spiritual activity governed by the Holy Spirit. A deeper examination of Scripture quickly reveals that the prophetic realm has different, and very distinct levels of operation and authority. An understanding of what these are can help you discover the level at which you operate. Best of all, knowing this can keep you from making major blunders in the prophetic realm.

Let me begin by saying that every vocal expression or spiritual activity is not prophecy, nor is it prophetic. There has been a great deal of unscriptural emphasis placed on the prophetic realm that started in the late 1970's and early 1980's. People have used the terms "prophecy" and "prophetic" for every activity of the Holy Spirit, and this improper use has really muddied the waters a great deal.

One group added even more confusion by calling every spoken word that hit the air "prophetics." Only God knows what that means, or where the term came from. Another group insisted that basically anything someone spoke was a "prophecy." Even worse, was a well-intended but unbiblical teaching based on one scripture that was pulled completely out of context that said, "…you all can prophesy…." As you read on, stay open and let the Holy Spirit bring much needed clarity to you in this wonderful, but greatly misunderstood realm.

Level 1
The Prophecy Of Scripture

The highest and most authoritative level of prophecy is the prophecy of Scripture. We read about this specific realm in 2 Peter 1:20-21 where it says:

"Knowing this first, that no prophecy of the scripture
is of any private interpretation. For the prophecy came
not in old time by the will of man: but holy men of God
spake as they were moved by the Holy Ghost."

2 Timothy 3:16 adds:

"All Scripture is inspired by God and profitable for teaching,
for reproof, for correction, for training in righteousness;"

The Greek word for "inspired" is *"theh-op'-nyoo-stos."* It means that something was divinely breathed <u>into</u> someone and thus it was given by literal inspiration or "breathing in" of the breath and life or "logos" of God. It is not something that has come out of the mind and imagination of man. For this reason the prophecy of Scripture has the highest level of authority.

Since Scripture has been "God breathed" it is the infallible standard by which all other prophecy must be evaluated and judged. Every prophetic word that is ever spoken must be measured directly against, and examined in the full light of Scripture. If anything contradicts God's established Word it has to be rejected, no matter how good it sounds. This is why Isaiah 8:20 says:

"To the law and to the testimony: if they speak not according to this
word, it is because there is no light (revelation of God) in them."

Any so-called prophetic word that does not align itself fully with the revelation of God's written Word has not been birthed out of the light of His presence. Words of this nature are soulish, earthly, natural and demonic in origin. They must be set aside no matter how good they sound, or true they may seem. God never contradicts Himself, and every valid prophecy will be in full agreement with the light and truth that is found in Scripture.

Needless to say, the Bible is a finished and complete work. When the Book of Revelation was written, that concluded the 66 books that were to become the canon of Scripture. It's interesting to note that the Greek word "canon" means "rule or measure, standard." In other words there was a specific measure used to determine each of the 66 Books that went into the Bible. Nothing else written or spoken meets that standard. Thus, there are no new books being added to it and no other writings or prophecies being considered as a companion for it.

No written or spoken prophecy will ever be on the same level of authority or truth, as the Bible. For this reason the Bible stands alone as the divine measuring rod by which we judge all other prophecy. Any group, religious organization or written material that tries to convince you otherwise is to be rejected. The Bible is a unique piece of literature being the only one that is prophetically confirmed as to it's accuracy and authenticity.

Level 2
The Canonical Prophets

The Bible was produced when God breathed His Word into specific men and women of old. They in turn were under the Spirit's direct influence and were moved by the Holy Spirit to actually speak or write what He was saying. 2 Peter 1:21 puts it this way:

> *"...For no prophecy was ever made by an act of human will,*
> *but men moved by the Holy Spirit spoke from God."*

The English word "moved" comes from a specific Greek word, which means, "to be borne up, driven or carried along." Canonical prophets were under the compelling force of the Holy Spirit as they spoke from and for God. They did this at a time when there was very little, if any, written Scripture. Because of this, the Old and New Testament canonical prophets were in a very special and unique group. Thus, the sixty-six books of the Bible are now a completed work and as such, the canonical prophets no longer exist. This is why all prophetic words spoken by modern prophets are not on equal ground with what was spoken by them.

The Old Testament canonical prophets were under the absolute letter of the law. This is because they were given the responsibility of being the only source of God's Word to His people. As a result, there was no room for error. In addition there was no mercy either, if a prophet was identified as a false prophet. In fact Scripture makes it very clear that a false prophet would soon be a dead prophet. Read Deut. 13:1-5, Deut. 18:20 and Jer. 28:15-17 below to recognize God's standard in this.

Old Testament prophets were under the law.

> *"If a prophet or a dreamer of dreams arises among you and gives*
> *you a sign or a wonder, and the sign or the wonder comes true,*
> *concerning which he spoke to you, saying, 'Let us go after other*
> *gods (whom you have not known) and let us serve them,' you shall*
> *not listen to the words of that prophet or that dreamer of dreams;*
> *for the LORD your God is testing you to find out if you love the*
> *LORD your God with all your heart and with all your soul.*

> *"You shall follow the LORD your God and fear*
> *Him; and you shall keep His commandments, listen*
> *to His voice, serve Him, and cling to Him.*

> *"But that prophet or that dreamer of dreams shall be put to*
> *death, because he has counseled rebellion against the LORD*

your God who brought you from the land of Egypt and
redeemed you from the house of slavery, to seduce you from
the way in which the LORD your God commanded you
to walk. So you shall purge the evil from among you.

"But the prophet who shall speak a word presumptuously in My
name which I have not commanded him to speak, or which he
shall speak in the name of other gods, that prophet shall die."

"Then Jeremiah the prophet said to Hananiah the
prophet, 'Listen now, Hananiah, the LORD has not sent
you, and you have made this people trust in a lie.'

"Therefore thus says the LORD, 'Behold, I am about to remove you
from the face of the earth. This year you are going to die, because
you have counseled rebellion against the LORD.' So Hananiah
the prophet died in the same year in the seventh month."

It should be noted that a false prophet was not simply a prophet who
was wrong. In Scripture, a false prophet could be a genuine prophet who
claimed to speak for God but actually counseled rebellion against Him.
They spoke in such a way that it caused the people to be led astray when
they had come to seek God's true counsel. Basically all false prophets
speak so as to seduce the people into following other gods, or in turning
away from the truth. Thus, God commanded that such evil should be
purged from among them.

A false prophet may also have been a follower of a false religion. As such,
they would be operating by a demonic spirit, and God expressly forbade
this as well. However, a false prophet can also be a genuine prophet of
God who is operating according to their own desires or stubborn will. At
times that happened simply because the prophet did not want to fall into

disfavor with the ruling king. It was easier to speak that which made the king happy, rather than that which would put their own life in jeopardy.

There is a reason why 1 Samuel 15:22-23 is in the Bible. Here we read:

"Has the LORD as much delight in burnt offerings and sacrifices as in obeying the voice of the LORD? Behold, to obey is better than sacrifice, and to heed than the fat of rams. For rebellion is as the sin of divination, and insubordination (stubbornness) is as iniquity and idolatry. Because you have rejected the word of the LORD, He has also rejected you ..."

These powerful words not only apply to King Saul, but they apply to prophets or anyone else who reject God's word. God says that rebellion and stubbornness against His word is the same as witchcraft and idolatry. When these are found in the heart of a genuine prophet, they have crossed over a deadly line. Their God-given ability to hear His voice has now become the very reason they are condemned. Because they are able to hear His voice, when they reject it, they are willfully identifying with all that is against Him, and that is a very dangerous place to be.

Rejecting God's voice is willfully identifying with all that is against God.

With the coming of Jesus, His blood made us right with God, and His grace and mercy are extended to all who are called to 5-fold ministry. Like it or not, that includes those in the office of the prophet. The New Testament prophet is not killed when they make a mistake, nor are they immediately branded as a false prophet. There is grace and mercy for those who miss it from time to time, and like all humans, New Testament prophets will make mistakes.

However, even in the New Testament when the individual was actually a false prophet, they did suffer consequences under the hand of God. We clearly see this recorded in Acts 13:6-11 (NASB):

> *"And when they had gone through the whole island as far as Paphos, they found a certain magician, a Jewish false prophet whose name was Bar-Jesus, who was with the proconsul, Sergius Paulus, a man of intelligence.*

> *"This man summoned Barnabas and Saul and sought to hear the word of God. But Elymas the magician (for thus his name is translated) was opposing them, seeking to turn the proconsul away from the faith.*

> *But Saul, who was also known as Paul, filled with the Holy Spirit, fixed his gaze upon him, and said, 'You who are full of all deceit and fraud, you son of the devil, you enemy of all righteousness, will you not cease to make crooked the straight ways of the Lord? And now, behold, the hand of the Lord is upon you, and you will be blind and not see the sun for a time.'*

> *"And immediately a mist and a darkness fell upon him, and he went about seeking those who would lead him by the hand."*

So, in the New Testament it's still not a free ride, and prophets can't do whatever they want. They have to know their God, feel His heart and reveal His will with accuracy and purity. There is grace, but it is closely coupled together with accountability. Even though there is the ability to clearly hear the voice of God, that ability can be hindered by human error. It's a mixture of heaven and earth that we have to contend with as long as we are in these mortal bodies.

Perhaps this is why the New Testament gives so much specific instruction on how prophets should function in the local church. Scripture also explains what to do with prophetic words, and it provides checks and balances to keep the ministry pure. As we examine the office of the New Testament prophet we will look more closely at these instructions, and the safeguards God put in place to protect His Church.

In closing this section, let's recap what has been said. With the death of Paul and John, and the writing of the Book of Revelation, Scripture was complete. No prophecy being spoken or written since then will ever be added to the Bible. All prophetic utterances made by modern prophets must be examined and lined up against the written Word of God. Prophecies that don't agree with Scripture are thrown out. However, we can thank God that the prophet who may have missed it is no longer killed in the process.

Levels 3, 4 & 5
God's Gifts To The Church

Each part of the Godhead gives specific gifts to the church. As we examine Scripture we can see what each gives and why. In fact 1 Cor. 12:4-7 clearly explains what each releases. In this passage we read the following:

> *"Now there are diversities of **gifts**, (Gk. "charisma") but the same Spirit (Holy Spirit). And there are differences of **administrations**, (Gk. "diakonia") but the same Lord (Jesus Christ). And there are diversities of **operations**, (Gk. "energema") but it is the same God (the Father) which worketh all in all."*
> *(Parenthesis and emphasis added.)*

Each part of the Godhead plays a specific role in releasing different gifts into the Church.

In the above Scripture we clearly see that each part of the Godhead plays a specific role in releasing different gifts into the Church. The Holy Spirit releases one kind (charisma), Jesus another (diakonia), and the Father yet another (energema). With this basic understanding in place let's take a quick look at what each part of the Godhead gives to the church as it relates to the prophetic realm.

First we see that the Holy Spirit releases a diversity of *gifts*. The word "charisma" is used here and it means a spiritual gift or supernatural enablement. 1 Cor. 12:6-9 mentions nine of these, but there most certainly are more than just these nine operating in the Church. We must remember that what is written in the Bible is not all there is to God. He is so much bigger than His Word. Scripture does reveal God to us, but it does not contain all that He is. John 21:25 explains it like this,

"And there are also many other things which Jesus did, which
if they were written in detail, I suppose that even the world
itself would not contain the books which were written."

A great example of this was related to me by a seasoned, well respected prophet/teacher of God named Steve Wilber. We were talking about this very thing and he explained that his mother had gotten saved and baptized in the Holy Spirit many years ago. One day she was praying in tongues and felt to grab a pencil and paper. To her surprise she began writing in a strange script. No one had any idea what it was until months later when missionaries from China came to their church. They recognized it, and when translated into English it was a clear word of the Lord. We see the finger of God writing on the wall in Daniel 5:27 and He wrote on tablets of stone in Exodus 31:18. Why is it so hard to believe that He might want to write through His Saints in this day?

The point is, however many gifts there may be, it's always just as the Holy Spirit wills. Each of the gifts is designed to reside within, be stirred up by, and flow through the believer for edification. We must never forget that the gifts are always for the building up of the Church. No matter how profound the gift may be, it's not about us. It's always about perfecting His Bride, the Church, until the day of His return.

Next we have the gifts that the Lord Jesus Himself, releases to His church. He gave different *administrations,* which is the Greek word "diakonia." This Greek word translates in Scripture as "offices, ministers, deacons and ministries." Ephesians 4:11-13 mentions five specific "ascension gift" ministries, or offices. Jesus gave these to the Church when He ascended back to heaven. They are for the building up and equipping of the Saints so they can do the work of the ministry. Today we call these the "five-fold" ministry, because there are five of them in all. These include the apostle, prophet, evangelist, pastor and teacher.

Finally we see that God the Father releases diversities of *operations.* This is the Greek word "energema" and it speaks of something that is actively at work within someone. This "energema" produces an effect or an inherent ability in the person. It is not something that lies dormant and then simply comes to life once in a while. It is more of an active force that is shaping the spiritual life and environment within the believer. The "energema" of the Father is in every believer to assist them, provide favor and shape their actual nature for some specific Kingdom purpose.

The word "worketh" is used in 1 Cor. 4:7 and it comes from a Greek word which means, "to show forth self." In other words, this "operation" that "worketh" in us is part of the package of life the Father placed within each person. It might be called the "gift of self" since it literally is the effect that the "energema" of God has on us as individuals. This is what causes us to actually view life a certain way. When connected to our personality, character traits and personal desires, it is the thing that makes us uniquely who we are. Thus the gift of the Father is one that makes each of us a unique, one-of-a-kind creation in God's Kingdom. By staying in communion with Him, our personal identity is fully uncovered and joyfully discovered.

The outworking of these three things produces a magnificent diversity and an amazing variety in the Body of Christ. No ministry or minister is exactly alike and each member of the Body functions best when it is connected to the part that compliments and completes it. Until we find our place, and connect to those who complete us, we will remain ineffective and unable to do all that God called us to do. This is exactly why every believer needs to be part of, connected to and actively involved in a good local church.

> **To be effective and do all God has for us requires connecting to those who complete us.**

This is also why it is such a waste when someone tries to mimic or copy the ministry or style of another minister. When we don't do things the way God designed them for us, we become nothing more than a cheap imitation. Let's face it, would you rather go and see the real Mona Lisa or a paint-by-number knock off of that masterpiece? Why then, would you want to settle for a paint-by-number ministry? Let the Lord develop the real you and then do what the old revivalists Charles Wesley did. Set yourself on fire for God and the people will come to watch you burn!

Many years ago, when I was a young worship leader, I saw Kent Henry, Lamar Boshman and Keith Green as the men to follow. They had great music, powerful messages and were setting the worship world aflame. So, in my zeal to excel I began to imitate them. I played the way they played, sang like they sang and even phrased words in my songs like they did. This worked at first, but in time I lost my passion for leading worship. Finally I lost myself and that was the real tragedy. I learned that when I was not who God made me to be, I was only a cheap imitation and it left me empty.

This design for a unique ministry style is exactly what Paul is speaking about in Romans 12: 4-5. Here we read:

"For just as we have many members in one body and all the members do not have the same function, so we, who are many, are one body in Christ, and individually members one of another. And since we have gifts that differ according to the grace given to us, let each exercise them accordingly ..."

As we really value and develop what God gave us, we can then connect to better serve the members of His body. Until the gifts, callings and abilities He placed in us find their genuine expression, we all operate at a much lower level than God intended. This is how He set up His Kingdom, and we need to embrace the principles that make it work. As long as we compare ourselves to another, and struggle with our own identity, we will fail to enjoy the diversity and uniqueness He built into each member of His body. In the final analysis, this is exactly what makes the devil happy. He knows better than anyone that a fake has no value. This is also why Paul wrote the following in 2 Cor. 10:12 (NKJV):

"For we dare not class ourselves or compare ourselves with those who commend themselves. But they, measuring themselves by themselves, and comparing themselves among themselves, are not wise."

Do yourself a big favor and take the time to discover the amazing things God placed within you. Learn to enjoy them and become who you really were designed to be in His kingdom. This is when the real value of who God made you to be will come out. A quote I once heard was, "you were born an original, don't die a copy." Better words of advice were never spoken. Find out why God made you, and what He anoints you to do. In so doing you have found the key to your high place in His Kingdom and will get great satisfaction from all that you do.

Old & New Testament Prophets

As we prepare to study the office of the prophet, remember what has already been said about the difference between the Old and New Testament prophet. Much of the confusion and misunderstanding about prophets and prophecy is due to the fact that people don't realize there is a distinct, and very important, difference between the old and the new covenant. Needless to say it is in understanding this distinction that removes all the conflict.

Old Testament Prophets were the only mouthpieces of God authorized to speak the Law.

To begin with, as was stated earlier, prophets under the old covenant lived by an absolute, God-given standard. They were not only under the Law but they were the only mouthpieces of God to speak that Law. They were a living, breathing Bible and as a result, mistakes were unacceptable. Beyond that, prophets who went into error, became rebellious, spoke presumptuously or spoke in the name of another god were considered false prophets and were killed.

Deuteronomy 18:20-22 is one of several key texts for Old Testament prophetic ministry that does not apply to the new covenant. It reads:

"But the prophet who shall speak a word presumptuously in My name which I have not commanded him to speak, or which he shall speak in the name of other gods, that prophet shall die."

The Hebrew word for presumptuously is *"zood"* and it means "to go beyond, to be insolent or to be proud." A true prophet could not go beyond what God was actually speaking. They had to deliver the Word exactly the way, and with the heart that God had, when He spoke it. Accordingly, the Old Testament standard for prophets was one without any mercy. If they were wrong they were dead!

Based upon Isaiah 8, Deuteronomy 18 and Jeremiah 23 we find these specifics given to us to identify true prophecy and false prophets in the Old Testament:

1. The word must line up with what was already written (Is.8:19-20).

2. The prophet could not speak in the name of another god (Deut. 18:20).

3. The prophet could not speak out of his own spirit or thoughts to lead people astray and make them believe a lie (Jer. 23:26-27, Jer. 28:15-17).

4. The prophecy must come to pass (Deut. 18:21-22).

5. The prophet could not go beyond what God had said or speak with a wrong, proud or insolent heart (Deut. 18:20-22).

There are some similarities between Old and New Testament prophets but the covenant under which the New Testament prophet operates is much different. Needless to say, anyone who speaks in the name of another God, or speaks in such a way as to lead people away from God, is still a false prophet. Joseph Smith and Jim Jones are two such examples. This kind of deliberate action always has deadly results. However, such actions are much different from the New Testament prophet who simply makes a mistake.

On occasion New Testament prophets do make mistakes. The fact is, every member of the five-fold ministry mentioned in Ephesians 4:10-11 are prone to mistakes. They are human and still "see through a glass darkly." In this case it does not make any of them false ministers. It does however serve to remind us that all ministers are human and all are made from the same dust. For this reason they need to be submitted under valid biblical authority to safeguard themselves and those they minister to.

This is also why we must never exalt any minister or ministry in this earthly realm. People will mess up, and we need to accept that as part of the human equation in spiritual things. As you read on, you will see the checks and balances God placed in His Word to protect the church, judge prophets and clarify the words they speak to His people.

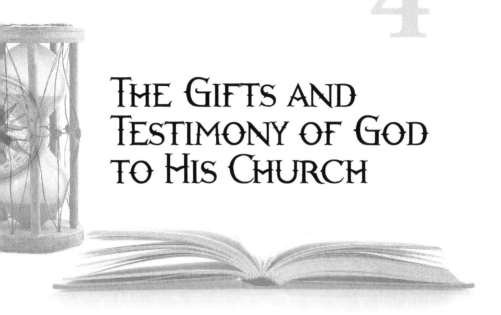

THE GIFTS AND TESTIMONY OF GOD TO HIS CHURCH

As was mentioned earlier, the first two levels of prophecy established God's Word to this Church. This happened through what was spoken by the canonical prophets and the actual written Word, which became our Bible. In this chapter we will take a much closer look at the second and third groupings of the prophetic. This will include the unique and special gifts that the Father, the Son and the Holy Spirit gave to the Church, and it will touch upon the power of our testimony when it is anointed by God.

Level # 3—The Gift Of Jesus To His Church
The Office Of The New Testament Prophet

New Testament prophets are set in place according to Ephesians 4:11-13. Jesus gave us them as a gift for the maturation of His Church. We also know that prophets today are not under the Law and they are not speaking forth what will become Scripture. Like any five-fold minister, they can and do make mistakes. When they do we should not brand them as false prophets. If we do, then we must also ask another very important question. Is a pastor who makes a mistake a false pastor? Is an evangelist who makes a mistake a false evangelist? Naturally the answer to these two questions is an emphatic, no!

Why is it then that many churches teach that a New Testament prophet must be without error? This standard is not from God and does not line up with His Word. New Testament prophets should never be expected to have 100% accuracy 100% of the time. Why? Because Jesus is the only human who was perfect. The rest of us are flawed in many ways. We don't always see things correctly and we need training, growth, mentoring, discipline and instruction on a continual basis. This is the nature of all humanity and it is a condition we all have to contend with.

New Testament prophets do make mistakes and God's Word has a provision for this very thing. Isn't that a good thing to know?

New Testament prophets do make mistakes, and God's Word has a provision for this very thing.

The New Testament gives a great deal of instruction to prophets on how they should work together and how every prophetic word should be judged. It is so specific, in fact, that Scripture tells believers to examine every prophetic utterance carefully and keep, or hold fast, that which is good. Apparently some utterances are not so good and these we should not hold on to. This is the instruction given in 1 Thes. 5:19-20. Here we read;

"Do not quench the Spirit; do not despise prophetic utterances. But examine everything carefully; hold fast to that which is good,"

Why would we have to examine everything (every prophetic utterance) carefully, and hold fast only to that which is good, if prophets were never wrong? We must conclude that sometimes what prophets say is not good.

Those things that are wrong we just throw out. Fortunately we are no longer instructed to throw the prophet out. If that were the case there would be very few prophets left in the Church.

A Personal Example

Prophet Kim Clement ministered in my wife's church in California on a regular basis over the years and we are very familiar with his ministry. He has made major predictions that have come to pass with pinpoint accuracy. Many times he has spoken very specific details about people's lives which impacted them deeply. He has accurately prophesied over movie stars, government officials and even the President of the United States. I deeply respect this man, his integrity and his ministry as a genuine prophet of God.

I have also prophesied over government leaders, church leaders and thousands of congregation members. On numerous occasions I prophesied over Pastors Charlie and Tammy Muller who are one of the major pastoral couples in Albany, New York. One time I prophesied over them about a major shakeup coming to the state government where corruption would be exposed. I also said they would be going on national television and that they would meet the governor of the state. Pastor Charlie actually laughed when I prophesied this because the words seemed so far out of reach. Not long afterwards corruption was indeed exposed at the Capital, Pastors Charlie and Tammy were interviewed on "Good Morning America" and they ate dinner with the Governor of New York State at the Governor's Mansion.

Even with consistent levels of accuracy like this Kim, myself and other genuine prophets have also made mistakes. This does not detract from our prophetic ministry, nor does it negate our callings as genuine prophets. However, it does serve to remind us that no matter how dynamic or accurate a prophet can be, we are nothing more than clay vessels that *"know in part and prophesy in part."* We all have to look to God's grace when we do make mistakes. Most of all, we have to get back up and keep going after we have missed it because this is the ministry God gave us and it must still be fulfilled through these flawed vessels.

This is one of the main reasons why it is so important every prophetic word spoken over someone be recorded and written out on paper, word-for-word. Local leadership will be the ones who have to deal with prophetic words, whether they come to pass or not. Because of this, every word must be taken to them for examination, confirmation and consultation. When things are not recorded or written down, very little of what is said will be correctly remembered. The basic policy I have is very simple. If a prophetic word is not recorded and written down, that word is lost and should be considered invalid.

A word left to memory will become so jumbled and mixed up in the mind of the hearer that for all practical purposes it is worthless. Our human tendency is to remember the high points, gloss over the places we don't like, and blend the rest together so that it says what we want it to say. However, a word that is recorded, written down and reviewed in detail by your church leadership will remain pure. It is not subject to personal interpretation, will not change, be glossed over or forgotten over time. This word can genuinely reveal your destiny and be used again and again to fight the good fight of faith. As you cherish this word, pray over it, and hold it up before the Lord it will help move you into your future, and that really pleases God.

Safeguards In Prophetic Ministry

It is important at this point to discuss a few safeguards when it comes to giving and receiving prophetic ministry. At this writing I have been functioning almost forty years as a prophet. Over that time I have identified some of the major problems that can arise. What follows are a few suggestions that will help you understand what these problems are, why they should be avoided, and how you can prevent such problems in your own life.

To begin with, any prophecy you receive must be spoken by someone who has the authority and the right to do so. Prophecy must always come through someone your leadership recognizes as having a valid ministry as a prophet. In addition, that prophet must be personally submitted under a valid apostolic oversight. If not, they are out of biblical order and have no right to speak into anyone's life. Such people have no checks and balances present in their ministry, and this is an unscriptural and dangerous thing for everyone.

People should never, and I mean never, embrace a "lone ranger" prophet no matter how gifted they are. God calls His Church to function in a spirit of interdependence, **not** independence. Unfortunately many embrace the latter and this has brought about division or "di-vision" (two visions) to the Body of Christ. Anything that brings division to His body is demonic in nature and should be avoided like the plague.

Along these same lines is another important reality. Any well-intentioned saint who gives a word to someone in private, apart from their leadership, is out of God's order. This kind of action is a major breach of pastoral trust. If what is said can't be said in front of your leadership, then it should never be said in the first place. Without the shepherd being present, the sheep have no protection. Remember, it's always the wolf that seeks to separate sheep from the safety of the flock. If anyone gives you a "wolf prophecy," reject it and run as fast as you can back to the safety of your shepherd!

The next thing to consider is the personal life of the one doing the prophesying. People with unproven ministry, emotional instability or undeveloped character have the potential of leaving a huge mess in those who listen to them. It can't be stated strongly enough that you should never make a life change, start a new ministry or be influenced in any way by a word from an unproven source. Feel free to listen, but never embrace or act upon a word given by someone like this. It could not only prove to be wrong, more than that it could prove to be deadly in the end.

If someone is going to speak into your life, be sure you have clear answers to all of the following questions. If you don't, my suggestion is to thank them for wanting to minister to you, but don't let them do it. Below are some prophetic ministry guidelines that I use.

Prophetic Ministry Checklist

1. Do they have validation by other proven prophets?

2. Are you going to record and write out what is spoken?

3. Are they submitted under valid apostolic authority?

4. Is the local leadership present when the word is spoken?

5. Will you go over this word with your leadership?

6. Does the person have proven good character?

7. Is the person emotionally and spiritually sound?

These are the most important questions you will ever ask when it comes to receiving a prophetic word. Without a clear "yes" to all of these, you are likely to end up getting a mess along with the message. When people don't meet these basic standards there is little protection, no guidance and an open door for the enemy to cause great confusion in your life. Worst of all, it can mess up everyone who trusts you and is following your example.

Level #4—The Gift Of Prophecy

The gift of prophecy is one of a number of spiritual gifts that God gave to His church through the Holy Spirit. The use and development of the gifts is mentioned in 2 Timothy 1:6. Here it says they reside within the person and should be "stirred up" on a regular basis. The words "stirred up" literally means to "kindle afresh" or "blow upon." This refers to how you would blow on a spark to start a fire. In other words, it is your responsibility to use the gifts God placed in you in order to keep them active and functioning. However it is the responsibility of your local leadership to develop those gifts so they will operate correctly, and at the right time.

It is your responsibility to use the gifts God placed in you in order to keep them active and functioning.

1 Timothy 4:14 goes on to say that we should not neglect any of the gifts within us. Amazingly enough it also states that these gifts can actually be imparted by the laying on of hands and prophecy of the presbytery. Perhaps this is one of the best reasons why the local church really needs the ministry of a prophetic presbytery team. When the team comes they may impart things of the Spirit that will actually change the spiritual level of the church, and this changes the people who are in it.

The gift of prophecy functions in a clearly defined way in the church. According to Scripture it is limited to a very specific level of operation. 1 Cor. 14:3 lists the parameters for it this way;

"But he that prophesieth speaketh unto men to edification, and exhortation, and comfort. ..." (KJV)

This gift is never used to provide correction, direction or any of the higher functions found in the office of the prophet. Those who step over the line and try to push into these realms are out of order and will cause harm and confusion to themselves and those they touch. However, the operation of the gift is still based upon the level of someone's faith. In fact all the gifts operate according to the level of faith people have. The more you believe God wants to use you, the more you will be open to Him doing so. This is why Hebrews 11:6 says:

> *"And without faith it is impossible to please Him, for*
> *he who comes to God must believe that He is, and*
> *that He is a rewarder of those who seek Him."*

The more you seek God to function in your gifts, the more He will reward your faith by letting them operate. In spite of the misuse of gifts by some, don't let that discourage you from using what God has given you. If you stay connected to your local leadership, pray in the Spirit and keep a humble, teachable attitude, you can be used in a powerful way as the gifts flow through you and out to others.

When Prophecy Is Not Prophecy

It should be noted that much of what is called "prophecy" in the church today is not prophecy at all. What is spoken is often one of the other vocal gifts and people incorrectly say, "I gave" or "I got" a prophecy. Just because something is spoken does not mean it is a prophecy. Prophecy, exhortation, the word of knowledge, the word of wisdom, tongues, interpretations of tongues and other verbal forms of edification are all vocal gifts. However, they are very distinct and separate operations of the Holy Spirit. To say every spoken word is "prophecy" is simply wrong.

I have found people don't often understand this basic concept. Even more confusing is that those who may be able to prophesy are not necessarily prophets. Teaching needs to be done on each of the gifts so people know which is which, and can understand what kind of "word" has been spoken. Is it a word of knowledge or a word of wisdom? Is it an interpretation or an exhortation? Perhaps it is a prophecy or even a word of encouragement. Once people really know which gift is in operation, a great many misunderstandings will be eliminated.

According to 1 Corinthians 14 the gift of tongues and the gift of interpretation of tongues, when used together, have the same effect as one who operates in the gift of prophecy. They both edify the church. Here we read;

> "One who speaks in a tongue edifies himself; but one who
> prophesies edifies the church. (5) Now I wish that you all spoke
> in tongues, but even more that you would prophesy; and greater
> is one who prophesies than one who speaks in tongues, unless
> he interprets, so that the church may receive edifying."
>
> 1 COR. 14:4-5 NASB

It's interesting to note that it says the one who prophesies is "greater" than the one who speaks in a tongue, unless that same person also interprets the tongue. The Greek word for greater is "meizon." It has the idea of something being more mature, greater in stature, more seasoned, older or at a higher level of development or faith.

What we learn from this is very important. Even though God has no favorites, it is clear that the gifts operate at different levels based upon our mastery of them and the level of our faith. Apparently it takes more faith to exercise the gift of prophecy than it does the gift of tongues, unless the gift of interpretation is also flowing in the same person. This is why 1 Corinthians 14:13 makes it clear that the interpretation of tongues is a priority when tongues happens in the church. Paul puts it this way;

> *"Therefore let one who speaks in a tongue pray*
> *that he may interpret." (NASB)*

In this sense, we could say that the joint operation of the gift of tongues and the gift of interpretation of tongues does the same thing, and requires the same level of faith, as the gift of prophecy. When operating together they fulfill God's design by functioning in the church to edify, exhort and comfort.

In studying the gift of prophecy we must always keep in mind that it has very clear parameters. It never rebukes, corrects, directs, causes division, speaks harshly or is released in anger. It does not give specific direction,

The gift of prophecy has clear guidelines.

release a ministry, speak about a life calling or unfold a revelation of the past, present or future. These deeper levels of prophecy only flow out of seasoned individuals who are in the office of the prophet. Those who are not prophets, and presumptuously speak to these levels, are in the flesh, or have been seduced by their own pride. They are simply moving by their own soulish nature and will accomplish nothing for God's Kingdom.

If someone in the church ever releases an incorrect word of this kind, it is very important for the leadership to step forward and bring gentle but firm guidance in the matter. The congregation will need to be informed of the error, and the one who gave it will need private instruction as well. This must be done in such a way that the sheep feel safe and the one in error is not humiliated, shamed or crushed.

God will give leaders wisdom in such cases, so that the church remains a safe place for people to grow, take risks and make mistakes. In this kind of environment it becomes easy for anyone to step out of their comfort zone and serve another while learning to operate in the gifts God put within them. Once fear of making a mistake is overcome, the gifts always operate more frequently and at a higher, more consistent level.

1 Corinthians 12:7 gives us a wonderful guideline for the proper expression of any of the gifts. It says:

> *"But to each one is given the manifestation*
> *of the Spirit for the common good."*

This means when a gift is exercised, it should always be for the good of the church, not for personal glory. I recommend that when a church sees the gifts flowing, someone should make note of them and record who did it and what specific gift was actually functioning. In this way different gifts can be identified and those who are moving in them consistently can be acknowledged and encouraged. This will serve to build the confidence of the people and stir them to use their gifts even more.

As you do this, the common good is promoted and people can be trained to use their gifts at the appropriate time and in the appropriate way. Under this kind of benevolent supervision all the gifts will begin to function more accurately and with greater consistency. Ultimately the entire church will be benefitted and the people will tend to grow and mature at a higher rate.

Gifts In The Church Service

The proper use of any gift is essential for it to benefit people in a church service. However, I have observed that this quite often does not happen. First of all, Spirit-filled Christians in general, have a hard time just sitting quietly in God's presence. At times God wants us to *"be still and know that I am God"* (Ps 46:10). When we meet for a service, and hit that deep, quiet place in worship, God often begins to stir the gifts within us. This is a good thing, and we all love it. However, the pattern we have embraced is to think that when we feel or hear something, it means we have to do or say something at that moment. This is because people don't understand the importance of just waiting quietly in God's presence so He can personally minister to them on an intimate, individual basis.

1 Cor 14:26 says that each can have a song, a word, a teaching or a revelation, but apparently that can cause confusion. This is because these things are often not being done properly and they do not benefit the church. Everything has to be done, especially the use of the gifts, so that the church is edified. The moment we hit that deep place in worship, and feel God stir within us, we usually think that is our cue to do or say something. Right or wrong that's what we all do and my question is, "Why"?

Now here is something most people don't realize, but the Lord showed me. When God shows up and we feel His presence, this will always make His gifts in us begin to stir. However, there are three (3) distinct possibilities of what is happening at that moment and people don't understand it. Below is a brief overview of the three things we need to consider.

✎ Possibility #1

God begins speaking to me and wants to minister that word privately, just to me during that quiet time. This means I should sit quietly in His presence and let Him do something within me that I personally need. When I feel God moving or speaking within me, why do I assume it's always right to take the microphone or that I have to do some other spiritual activity? What if God simply desired to speak personally to me? Due to incorrect training, or lack of understanding, I can speak or use any gift I have when it was supposed to be something just between God and me.

✦ Possibility #2

God begins speaking to me about what He is doing with everybody in that service. Once again, why do I have to broadcast that? It is an intrusion into God's intimate personal ministry to His church if I speak at this time. So, when I feel God moving in that instance and my gifts get stirred up, it is just not the time to speak. No one needs to tell the church what God is doing with His Bride. It's another spiritual habit we all have picked up and done in ignorance on a regular basis.

Look at it this way. If Wendy and her husband are sitting on a couch in a very quiet, private, intimate embrace, do they need or even want someone to stand up, grab a microphone and say "Wendy and her husband are now in a private intimate embrace on the couch." Of course not! That would be an unnecessary intrusion into a private moment. It simply did not need to be explained. However, this tends to be done all the time in church services. When it happens, it actually robs the people of a moment of united corporate intimacy He desired. How often has this happened in your church services?

Think about this for just a moment. God begins to move on the congregation and we all come to this quiet, deep place in worship. Next thing you know somebody feels their gift being stirred, so what do they do? They grab the microphone and tell the church what they all know He is doing. My question to all of us is, "Why?" Speaking at this time is an invasion into the personal corporate relationship God intended to have with His Bride and it should not happen.

When we do this, it literally robs the church as a body from experiencing the Lord together. We actually get between the Lord and His people. It's just another religious tradition that we have adopted. I believe it grieves the Holy Spirit when we act like children and do something just because we are emotionally stirred up. Mature, well-instructed saints should know the difference, and be able to honor what God is doing in others without intruding into that sacred moment.

ଛ Possibility #3

God is actually speaking to me and wants me to share what He is saying to the Church. When I speak in this moment I edify those who need it and bring focus to those who have missed what God is actually doing. At times people do miss what God is in the process of doing, and a spoken word, or a gift used at that specific moment gives everyone correct focus and needed clarity. This is when we definitely need to speak out and share God's heart. It is the perfect order for that moment in the service because it edifies the church as God intended.

What Does All This mean?

From a biblical perspective, this means two out of three times our gifts are stirred in service it requires us to say or do nothing. We should all get comfortable in waiting in His presence to see what He is doing and wants us to do. Do you remember why He gave us the Holy Spirit? The Holy Spirit is the great Teacher who gives us all revelation and direct access to the things of God. It is always better to wait a little and allow the Spirit to provide us with clear direction, then to use our gift improperly only to hijack a service.

Often we unintentionally step between God and His Bride just so we can use our gifts. When we do this we rob the people of the opportunity they need to hear from the Lord themselves and hearing His voice is really what God has always wanted. Like it or not, every time someone takes the microphone, people stop focusing on the Lord and they focus on that person. It can be the perfect thing to do, or it can be an invasion into what God was already doing. When we miss it, we pull everyone away from an intimate encounter with the Lord, and it brings the focus on something else. People simply need to be instructed on how to properly use their gifts so that they draw others into, and not away from, God's presence.

A Demonic Counter Part

Since the devil cannot produce anything out of his own creative ability, he is forced to simply imitate and corrupt what God is doing. This serves to distract, misdirect and confuse those who come in contact with his deceptions. The greatest example of this today is the current fascination with psychic hot lines, new age fairs, crystal healing, fortunetellers, palm readers and the like. As one begins to really examine how these counterfeits operate, the shallowness of their activity becomes very apparent.

The Bible tells us that God made every person to be something specific before they were even born. Jeremiah 1:5 and Isaiah 49:1 say:

> *"Before I formed you in the womb I knew you,*
> *And before you were born I consecrated you; I have*
> *appointed you a prophet to the nations."*

"Listen, O coastlands, to Me, And take heed, you peoples from afar! The Lord has called Me from the womb; From the matrix of My mother He has made mention of My name."

Thus the blueprint of God was established for Jeremiah, Isaiah and for every person, before birth. The spiritual equipment needed to fulfill that blueprint is within everyone as well. No matter what they do with their life, God does not change His mind about His design for them. Romans 11:29 says: *"for the gifts and the calling of God are irrevocable."* Because of this fact, it does not matter if the person comes to Christ, or if they don't serve God at all. The gifts He gave them are still in them, and they will seek to find their full expression in that person's life.

This is the very reason Proverbs 22:6 says we should train up a child *"in the way he should go,"* so when that child matures they will not depart from it. The phrase "in the way he should go" is actually translated in the Hebrew as "according to his bent," that is according to the nature God put in him. That understanding alone sheds new light on an important issue. Namely, that God placed in every human a personal design with specific gifts. These will help them most effectively do what they were created to do. Thus the main job of parents is to discover what that design is so they can guide and train their children accordingly.

God placed in every human a personal design with specific gifts.

The true design of God will always manifest as a cry in the heart that seeks to find satisfaction and fulfillment. If one is designed to be a teacher, they will naturally break down things so that they are clear and easy to be understood. Built into them is the apparatus to do this. In like fashion, one with the gift of mercy will automatically cry out for and seek to help the hurting. It is something in them that will not rest and yearns to be satisfied.

We can see this same principle in the creation of Satan himself. Ezek. 28:13-14 says it best. Here we read;

> "Thou hast been in Eden the garden of God; every precious stone was thy covering, the sardius, topaz, and the diamond, the beryl, the onyx, and the jasper, the sapphire, the emerald, and the carbuncle, and gold: the workmanship of thy tabrets and of thy pipes was prepared in thee in the day that thou wast created. {14} Thou art the anointed cherub that covereth; and I have set thee so: thou wast upon the holy mountain of God; thou hast walked up and down in the midst of the stones of fire."

Verse 13 says that the workmanship of his tambourines and flutes (musical instruments) were prepared in him on the day he was created. Since his design was to lead worship in the heavens, what he needed in order to do his job was a part of his very being. This nature functioned through him and found expression for the purpose of exalting God's Glory.

Since the gifts and callings of God are irrevocable, when satan fell, his gifts fell with him. Today we can see the results of that fall all over the earth. It is expressed in the kind of music being created by unsaved musicians. They are using the gifts God gave them to produce songs that are filled with hate, death, lust, darkness and perversion.

Every gift from God is good, but the heart of the one using it may not be. When anyone operates in the gift God built into them, they will do so to satisfy the cry from within. If they find the Lord, they will tune into the Holy Spirit and be led by Him into spiritual revelation and truth. The gifts will develop in them and try to excel along those lines. However, those who reject God still have their gifts, but they will now be connected to and empowered by an ungodly, demonic source. These gifts will now develop and excel along those lines.

What unsaved people can be led by, and who they receive things from, can be God, but most often it is demonic or natural, and they don't realize it. This causes a real problem for the one who is not saved but is called to be a prophet. Remember, they still have all the spiritual apparatus to see and hear into the spiritual realm, but they will be plugged into the wrong spiritual source most of the time. Because of this, what gets released through them will be a reflection of that dark spiritual world.

Contrary to popular teaching, those who do not know God can hear from Him. In fact, every unsaved person must be able to hear God or they could never be saved in the first place. Ungodly people actually do hear from God through dreams and divine visitation on occasion. Take for example King Darius and King Nebuchadnezzar. Both were given divine revelations from God but neither knew Him. Rest assured that demonic spiritual powers will see to it that the expression of gifts in the unsaved will find their source in the demonic realm. This is to assure that the gifts are perverted and funneled back to promote and empower the world system.

God's gifts always cry out to function for what they were created to do. They will manifest in everyone, one way or another. As a result, the word of knowledge, word of wisdom, apostolic gift, teaching gift, creative gifts, those with a gift for finances, even the gifts of mercy or administration will all seek to find their full expression even in those who are not serving God. These people will find false satisfaction by using their gifts while being plugged into the wrong source.

> **God's gifts always cry out to function for what they were created to do.**

Many in the entertainment industry have fame by learning how to use their God-given gifts. However, the enemy also knows how to redirect those gifts as well. What has recently come to light demonstrates this very thing. Many entertainers say that something comes over them when they hit that high place of excellence. Singers and actors alike mention that something just takes them over and they are able to do amazing things that are beyond their natural ability. Actor Robin Williams, who just committed suicide, and singer Beyonce have both stated that they become another person and feel something take them over when they perform. In other words, the gifts God gave them have been successfully high-jacked by a demonic source.

From that perspective, you can begin to understand how the devil takes advantage of something God intended for the Kingdom. Perhaps we all should look at those in the world who have such profound gifts in a different light. Why not ask the Holy Spirit to help you see them with God's eyes. He can show how to bring them in with the harvest that is crying out to find Christ in the darkness. These people have simply learned to use the gifts God placed in them but they are not evil. They are living a very successful, counterfeit life, but they are still loved and wanted by God.

Relationship & Revelation Vs. Knowledge & Information

Man was designed to live in relationship with God, and receive revelation by the Spirit. When man fell, he exchanged relationship for knowledge and revelation for information. Rather than eating from the tree of life, he chose to eat from the tree of the knowledge of good and evil. He fell from a spiritual place of walking with God and knowing Him personally, into a soulish, demonic realm where God was feared and kept at a distance. All men have been born into this lower realm ever since.

This pattern is what got Jacob into so much trouble. He would not wait for God to give him revelation on how he would receive the promised birthright and the blessing. Instead, he got information from his mother and stole it by deception. In a similar way, this is exactly how psychics operate. They use known information from the spirit realm and masquerade it as revelation to unsuspecting people. It's basically one big deception designed to suck people into the dark world of the occult. The built-in spiritual curiosity we all have is the perfect hook to catch the naïve, and trap those who are ignorant of the demonic realm.

Recognize first of all that satan and his demons are not omnipresent or omniscient. They are not an equal power to God, and they do not know everything that is going on. They have no understanding of God's Word and have no revelation about the future. The only thing they do know is what has happened in the past and what is happening in the present. They have information about what they have witnessed or they can be told what other demons have witnessed.

More importantly, they study and know human nature and that is made very clear when you consider what happened when satan came to accuse Job. The devil and his demons know how the soul and flesh of man responds under certain circumstances. Since they understand how man's mind, will, emotions and nature operate, they are masters at manipulating people by these things. It is through this knowledge, and man's curiosity with the spiritual, that the enemy finds fertile ground for his cheap deception to operate.

What really happens with a true psychic is very simple. They have a gift from God, but it is connected to the wrong spiritual source. Romans 1:21 says they have rejected the knowledge of God and their hearts have now become darkened. God gives them over to a reprobate mind to do those things that are not right. In this spiritually darkened state God's gift still works but it now connects to the demonic realm where information and knowledge are easily available. With this in mind, let us look at how these pieces fit together to fool the innocent, trap the ignorant and put the unsuspecting in emotional bondage to the occult.

How Do Psychics Operate?

In our example we find Sue somewhat distressed so she calls a psychic hot line. When she calls she is told the following: "You have been having money problems but in a few days you will get a check. Money will come for the new car you need. Also your uncle has died and he says he's fine." When Sue hears these words she is absolutely amazed. She hangs up and calls her aunt to find that her uncle has indeed died several days ago. She is also astonished because she knows she has been having financial problems and really does need a car.

As Sue thinks about it, she realizes there is no way the psychic could have possibly just guessed all this. She is convinced that the psychic is the real deal and can't wait to talk to them again. To her absolute shock, a check for $15,000 actually arrives in the mail three days later just like the psychic said. It came from her uncle who left her the money when he died. This so astonishes Sue that she tells everyone she knows about the psychic and how "right on" they were. Though she does not realize it, Sue has just become a new convert to the occult. The question we are forced to ask at this point is "What really went on here?"

Most people would say that the psychic did know the future and did talk to the dead uncle. After all, the uncle was dead and Sue did get the money just like the psychic said. Isn't this telling the future? The answer is absolutely no! The psychic did not know the future nor did they talk to the dead uncle. In essence, this is nothing more than a very cheap, spiritual deception. Yet there is a supernatural element to what went on and this is what sucks people in.

Demonic Communication And Control

The truth is very simple in the above situation and it is rooted in the invisible, spiritual world. What we find is that demonic spirits have heard Sue talking about her finances for months. She's been broadcasting that every place she has gone, and the spirit world has heard it. Other demons have been nearby when her car broke down and they were there when she looked for a car. No revelation here, just information that these entities have witnessed or been told.

Demonic spirits can hear what we broadcast. When we provide them with information, it is not spiritual revelation.

In another part of the country other demonic spirits know her uncle has been sick. It may have even been under their devilish influence that he got sick and died. The thing is Sue does not know any of this. First of all Sue does not see into the spirit realm and she is not aware of the demonic forces that are in the atmosphere. The spirits know her but she is unaware of them and lacks this spiritual understanding. Secondly, her aunt had not yet told her that the uncle was dead so she also lacked that knowledge. Keeping all this in mind, let's take a look at just how this demonic deception works.

To begin with, specific demons saw the uncle die and they saw a check being mailed out to Sue. Others have heard Sue tell people about her financial need and they know all about her search for a car. Thus, nothing the psychic says along these lines is spiritual revelation. It is simply information that has been communicated and passed along through the demonic spiritual realm. One demon passes the information along to the next. A true psychic has learned how to use the apparatus God gave them to get this information from the spiritual realm. They then speak it out to those who have paid to hear it.

Psychic healing is the same type of deception. In the demonic realm, everything is about power and control. There is a demonic hierarchy identified in Ephesians 6:12 that is listed as *"rulers ... powers ... world forces of this darkness ... spiritual forces of wickedness in heavenly places."* In this realm the strongest demon always controls those that are weaker. To bring "healing," a psychic healer must operate with a demon that is stronger than the one causing the disease. The weaker demon will temporarily be controlled and must give way to the stronger authority. When this happens the weaker demon simply shifts to another organ or becomes dormant. Thus the person thinks they have been cured when in fact the problem has only been disguised, covered over or gone dormant.

In time the sickness will return again and this is a double benefit to the psychic. The sick person must continue to go back again and again to stay healed and so the psychic is making a lot of money. This will continue as long as they can keep up the appearance of doing something good, while actually using evil to do it. Remember, satan will not cast out satan because he knows a kingdom divided against itself cannot stand. The weaker demon simply continues to be subjugated and controlled by the stronger one, but it is not cast out.

Eventually one of several things must happen. The weaker demon will either leave, or it will remain subjugated and invade other areas. As long as it is there, the stronger one must continue to exert energy to control it in order to keep up the appearance of a continued healing. Once the weaker demon can no longer be controlled, or the money runs out, the party is over, the disease returns and they die anyway.

The diagrams that follow show in a very simple format exactly what is gong on with Sue. As you examine this be sure to keep in mind that there is a supernatural element involved, but it is not God. 2 Thes. 2:11 talks about this very thing. Those who want the supernatural but reject God will still get power, but it will be a counterfeit. This is why it says:

"And for this reason God will send upon them a deluding influence so that they might believe what is false."

Once people reject what is true the only thing left is a lie. No matter how nice it is dressed up, or how it may touch someone, it's still deception and can't really benefit them in the end.

The demonic influence that is present in the life of psychics becomes very clear when you discover how their final days are spent. The inborn nature and fascination with spiritual things was a gift from God. However, fulfilling that desire the wrong way was a trap that destroyed them in the end. Since the devil knows how to draw upon, manipulate and entice the unsaved into using God's design in their life, in time they are caught in something that will ultimately be to their destruction.

> **We were born with a fascination for spiritual things. This is God's nature in us.**

Take a moment to look over the diagrams on the next page. See if you can understand how this all works. Our best defense is to know the truth, and in love share that truth with those who need it. Once you understand what follows, you will be able to easily rescue anyone from the lie of the enemy. You may be used to deliver some who are actually designed to be mighty men and women of God. What a privilege it would be to snatch them from the jaws of death, and bring them into the Kingdom of God's Love.

What follows is a brief overview of the devil's cheap deception. Study it and take what you learn with you. When you encounter those who have been touched by this deception you will have the tools you need to set them free!

The Case Of Sue

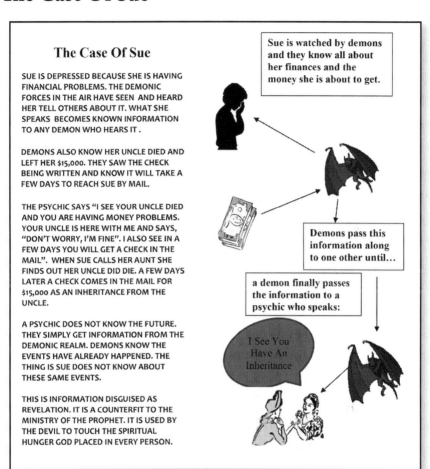

Tragically, most Christians are unaware of such deception and the devil has been using it for years. The church has been so lacking in true character, clear teaching and spiritual power that people are more in fear of the occult than they are willing to encourage and believe God's prophets. It will take a mature prophetic people, who know their place in God, to expose what is false and demonstrate the truth. Once this happens, satan's cheap tricks will come down like a house of cards, and the church will rise up as God intended. My prayer is that this next great awakening will unleash the truth with such power and clarity that it can't be counterfeited and won't be denied.

Level # 5—The Grace Gift Of Prophecy

I believe there is a fifth level of the prophetic that is mentioned in Scripture. This prophetic gift functions according to Romans 12:6. It is an operation of God the Father's grace in an individual's life. I call this the "grace gift" of prophecy. The grace gifts are those that actually motivate people in certain ways in life. They are a part of the package of life each person has received from the Father. These gifts connect with the personality, natural gifts, temperament and character of the person to give them a frame of reference for how they view life.

Romans 12:6 puts it this way:

> *"And since we have gifts that differ according to the grace given to us, let each exercise them accordingly: if prophecy, according to the proportion of his faith;"*

Thus we see that these gifts all differ according to the "grace" given to us for their operation. They are a supernatural endowment that gives one a certain point of view and a level of divine favor in specific areas of life. The word "grace" that is used here means "a divine influence upon the heart that reflects in the natural life."

As previously mentioned, 1 Cor. 12:6 uses the Greek word *"energema"* for these gifts and they come from the Father. When studied out, the Greek word *"energema"* comes from a root word that means, "to show or disclose self," These gifts are part of who we are and how we disclose or show forth ourselves to the world around us.

They influence how we view our own place in life and how we may view the actions and needs of others.

What Are The Grace Gifts?

The grace gifts are those splashes of divine influence that are built within us by God. These motivate us and give us favor or an extra edge in daily life, depending on their influence. They operate in everyone as an inherent ability that is given to them as part of the package of life from the Father. In a sense, these gifts act like lenses through which we see life. They energize and motivate us in very specific ways. This explains why some people seem to be natural leaders while others find success and great joy in serving, showing mercy or providing instruction to those who need it. The grace gifts within them lean them towards a specific predisposition and place of favor.

Every grace gift will operate through the God-given natural abilities, talents, and temperaments that are built into us. Once we know what gifts are present, we can learn to focus on them and flow with them. This will provide us with an advantage and can give us favor in specific circumstances on the job, with friends, family or in the community. There are a number of grace gifts listed in Romans 12:6–9 and they all operate according to a specific design from God. They include prophecy, serving, teaching, exhortation, giving, leadership, mercy and love.

Grace gifts include: prophecy, serving, teaching, exhortation, giving, leadership, mercy and love.

Romans 12 says the grace gifts function best in the parameters set in place for them in Scripture. In the case of prophecy, it functions best according to the measure, and in relationship to the faith we have. The gift of giving works best when it is done with liberality, joy and generosity. According to Romans 12:8, the gift of leadership works best when released from a humble heart, with pure motives, and when it is done with all diligence. As you identify the grace gift God placed in you, and nurture it correctly, it will be a benefit to you in many ways throughout your life.

This explains why our perception of life, and the life circumstance of others, will really determine how we respond to any given situation. If Tom is having a financial problem and he speaks to one with the grace gift of mercy, this person will seek to comfort him. If he goes to one with the grace gift of liberality they may want to take up an offering. One with the grace gift of teaching will give him a list of Scriptures to stand upon and set up a study on how to resolve the conflict. The point is, everyone will be motivated to respond according to the operation of the gifts that are in them, and this can create some interesting conflicts at times.

The Prophetic Grace Gift

What I have seen is that the prophetic grace gift gives people insight in difficult situations. One who has this gift will often see life through a lens of absolutes. Things will appear to be right or wrong, black or white and there will be very little gray area in their point of view. It provides clarity in confusing circumstances and will often allow someone to make good decisions, or provide clear direction when others are not sure about what to do next.

Needless to say this will also provide someone with a distinct advantage in many circumstances. It can keep the person in a favorable light for job advancement and may put them in line ahead of others for personal promotion. The down side of the gift is that people with it may often become critical, impatient and judgmental of others. Those who don't see things as clearly or as quickly as they do may be cut off, run over or ignored all together. Conflict will often arise with those who are more methodical and want all the facts spelled out before they are willing to proceed.

People with this gift can often make decisions with little or no planning and this will be very disturbing for those that have to work or live with them. This can irritate, frustrate and cause those around them to feel very insecure because of their impulsive nature and their ability to change direction because of a "gut feeling." All of this can happen, and they may not even be aware of the emotional discomfort they have caused.

Naturally, each of the other gifts also presents their own set of problems. Those who have the grace gift of mercy will tend to view those who have the prophetic grace gift as being overbearing, impatient, impulsive, judgmental or authoritative. Those who have the grace gift of liberality may see those with an administrative gift as stingy, selfish, a nitpicker and even greedy. This is because the one with liberality will find great joy in giving while those with the gift of administration will tend to be more calculating and number oriented in what they give. They will have a much higher need for certainty and tend to be more fact oriented, detailed and organized about what and to whom they give.

Each gift has strengths. Each gift also presents its own set of problems.

Professions that would benefit from those with a prophetic grace gift would be those involving the need for clarity and accuracy in changing circumstances. This would include such professions as lawyers, detectives and police. Teachers would benefit from the insight a prophetic grace gift gives as they deal with the changing needs of students. Doctors, social caseworkers and counselors would also have a distinct advantage if this gift were in them.

There are many applications that could be suggested, however, the point is, the prophetic grace gift provides insight, clarity and solution directed resolutions. If this seems to be a natural ability you have, there is a good chance that the grace gift of prophecy is one the Father has built into your life's blueprint. This is the real source of where intuition comes from that you may experience from time to time. When we are in critical situations, the grace gift of prophecy along with the gift of discernment will kick into gear and operate together as a source of protection.

Learning to recognize the gift when it happens is a tremendous help in any situation. Begin to ask God to show you what grace gifts are built into your nature. As He does, life will take on a whole new meaning, and the advantage you have by learning to use these gifts will become evident very quickly.

If the grace gift of prophecy is in you, and you begin to look at life through this prophetic lens, it will bring things into right perspective. When this is consistently demonstrated, you will be known as one who makes clear, focused decisions in confusing situations. Be encouraged to work with it, develop it and rely upon it. As you exercise the measure of faith you have in this gift, it will serve you better. You will see it increase and become a source of great blessing in daily life and to those around you.

Level # 6—The Spirit Of Prophecy

The spirit of prophecy has a specific function in the Church and I have discovered that it operates several different ways. First of all it may fall on a congregation when there is a high level of praise and worship. When this happens, the spirit of prophecy will influence people to speak when they may never have spoken out before. Most likely this will be a general exhortation to the church and it will always operate in perfect alignment with the atmosphere of the meeting. Frequently the gift of tongues and interpretation may be flowing freely at the same time.

The easiest way to recognize the spirit of prophecy is to look for people who begin to speak out that normally don't. If they are speaking according to the flow of the service, that is most likely the spirit of prophecy. In essence, the spirit of prophecy is the testimony of Jesus as He speaks through people, about what He is doing or feeling for His church at that moment. Rev 19:10 says:

> *"And I fell at his feet to worship him. And he said to me,*
> *'Do not do that; I am a fellow servant of yours and your*
> *brethren who hold the testimony of Jesus; worship God.*
> *For the testimony of Jesus is the spirit of prophecy.'"*

If Jesus wants to testify about His church, or to His church, the spirit of prophecy will come to do just that. When it happens, people need to relax and enjoy listening to the Lord as He speaks to and through His people. Remember, those who may never have opened their mouths in service before will do so with ease when the spirit of prophecy comes. As that begins it is a huge faith builder for the whole congregation.

In the Old Testament, the spirit of prophecy is often connected to some element of praise and worship. 1 Sam. 10:5-7 and 2 Kings 3:15 are good examples of this. Here we read:

> *"'Afterward you will come to the hill of God where the*
> *Philistine garrison is; and it shall be as soon as you have*
> *come there to the city, that you will meet a group of prophets*
> *coming down from the high place with harp, tambourine,*
> *flute, and a lyre before them, and they will be prophesying.*

'Then the Spirit of the LORD will come upon you mightily, and
you shall prophesy with them and be changed into another man.

"And it shall be when these signs come to you, do for yourself
what the occasion requires; for God is with you.

'But now bring me a minstrel.' And it came about, when the
minstrel played, that the hand of the LORD came upon him."

As you can see, the spirit of prophecy may come upon individual people or whole congregations. Anyone He rests upon has the ability to speak the heart of God. Those who speak out may never do it again, but at

Anyone God rests on has the ability to speak His heart.

that moment they can launch right out with ease. You will here the Lord speaking through the most unlikely people as He builds up, edifies, exhorts and encourages His church. Because of this it will never be a rebuke or a correction, and it will not set a new direction for the service. In addition we never see in Scripture that it produces personal, one-on-one prophecy. That is a function of the office of the prophet or occasionally the gift of prophecy.

Another example of the spirit of prophecy is found in Numbers 11:25. Here we read;

"Then the LORD came down in the cloud and spoke to him; and
He took of the Spirit who was upon him and placed Him upon
the seventy elders. And it came about that when the Spirit rested
upon them, they prophesied. But they did not do it again."

Several other examples are found in 1 Samuel 10:10 and 1 Samuel 19:20. These read:

*"When they came to the hill there, behold, a group of prophets
met him; and the Spirit of God came upon him mightily, so
that he prophesied among them. And it came about, when all
who knew him previously saw that he prophesied now with
the prophets, that the people said to one another, 'What has
happened to the son of Kish? Is Saul also among the prophets?'"*

*"Then Saul sent messengers to take David, but when they saw
the company of the prophets prophesying, with Samuel standing
and presiding over them, the Spirit of God came upon the
messengers of Saul; and they also prophesied. And when it was
told Saul, he sent other messengers, and they also prophesied.*

*So Saul sent messengers again the third time, and they
also prophesied. Then he himself went to Ramah, and
came as far as the large well that is in Secu; and he asked
and said, 'Where are Samuel and David?' And someone
said, 'Behold, they are at Naioth in Ramah.'*

*"And he proceeded there to Naioth in Ramah; and the
Spirit of God came upon him also, so that he went along
prophesying continually until he came to Naioth in Ramah.*

*"And he also stripped off his clothes, and he too prophesied
before Samuel and lay down naked all that day and all that
night. Therefore they say, 'Is Saul also among the prophets?'"*

Needless to say Saul was not among the prophets but he could speak prophetically when the spirit of prophecy came upon him. So it is with all those who are under the influence of the spirit of prophecy. When He comes, the meekest person in the church can open their mouth to testify or declare with boldness what God is doing. Under the spirit of prophecy anyone can become a mouthpiece for Jesus as He speaks the testimony of what He is doing in His Church.

As seen in the scriptures above, when the spirit of prophecy comes upon an individual or a congregation the level of prophetic operation tends to be greatly enhanced. I have seen those who have the gift of prophecy and those in the office of the prophet begin to operate at a higher level once the spirit of prophecy came into a meeting. Perhaps this is why Scripture said of Jesus *"the Spirit of the Lord is upon me ..."* Operating in the spirit of, rather than the gift of, is moving in a whole different realm of power and anointing.

It is recorded that William Branham would often wait for the moving of the spirit of prophecy before he would begin to minister. Once it came, and he sensed the direction things were going, there were amazing operations of the Spirit that took place in his meetings. Prophetic words, healings, visions and revelations came that exceeded what happened in the Book of Acts. He knew the difference and realized it was important to wait for that higher realm of anointing. Perhaps we should relax, wait on God and do the same.

When the spirit of prophecy is present, a higher realm of anointing is available.

Aspects Of The Spirit Of Prophecy

Our personal testimony has that prophetic element to it. The written Word of God is the truth, the testimony of what God has already done for the Church and it has a prophetic anointing on it. So also, our personal testimony has a prophetic anointing because it is also the truth, the true record of what God has done for us, in our life. Our testimony is truth that the enemy cannot change. Telling it releases the spirit of prophecy and this is why it can impact, soften and penetrate those who hear it.

As we testify to what God has done, the spirit of prophecy comes upon our words to pierce the heart of anyone who hears what we say. This is why it is very important to speak the absolute truth as you share your personal testimony. Since this will be the framework through which the spirit of prophecy operates, giving an "embellished" testimony will grieve the Spirit and He will not anoint our exaggerations. This will bring death just as surely as false prophecy brings trouble to those who give and receive it.

Personal testimony is so powerful that the Bible says this about it in Rev. 12:11:

> *"And they overcame him because of the blood of the*
> *Lamb and because of the word of their testimony,*
> *and they did not love their life even to death."*

The prophetic anointing on personal testimony carries the power to defeat and overcome the devil in any situation. Even the youngest Christian can use their testimony in a powerful way knowing the spirit of prophecy anoints it. What a great thing to know and take advantage of in our fight of faith. This is why Psalms 78:4 says:

> *"We will not conceal them from their children, But tell to*
> *the generation to come the praises of the LORD, And His*
> *strength and His wondrous works that He has done."*

This is also why the man with the legion of demons had such a profound impact on his region. After Jesus healed him of the demonic possession, he was instructed to do something very simple. The man wanted to follow Jesus but instead we are told this in Mark 5: 19-21:

> *"And He did not let him, but He said to him, 'Go home to*
> *your people and report to them what great things the Lord has*

> *done for you, and how He had mercy on you.' And he went
> away and began to proclaim in Decapolis what great things
> Jesus had done for him; and everyone marveled. And when
> Jesus had crossed over again in the boat to the other side, a great
> multitude gathered about Him; and He stayed by the seashore."*

When you testify to what God has done in your life, it is God's truth and it is filled with His life and power. Just like the testimony of Jesus, your testimony also carries a prophetic anointing upon it. No devil in hell can deny or stop those words since they are the truth of what Jesus did for you personally. This is one of the major weapons we can use to overcome the devil, no matter how he attacks us in life.

Your testimony is God's truth to you and carries a prophetic anointing on it.

Keep this in mind as you tell others about what Jesus has done for you. Look for that prophetic anointing to be on your words and watch them penetrate the resistant heart, soften the hard heart and melt the cold heart. Your testimony, which is really the testimony of Jesus in your life, can make a huge difference in those who hear it. It can be the key that unlocks people, releases healing and sets the captive free.

A good presentation should be from the heart, no longer than five minutes and filled with your personal story. It should speak about life before you met Jesus, what happened the day you got saved and what life is like now. Just be honest, truthful and genuine. These are the things that touch people and make them want to listen to you. It's not about being fancy or filling in every last little detail. It's about what God has done in you and how you are different now that He is living in your heart.

Let me suggest that you take the time to first write out your testimony. Keep it simple and don't load it up with numerous details or endless sidetracks that distract from what really happened. Begin to practice telling your story to those you know. Ask for constructive criticism, suggestions and personal insights on how to make it better. Once you have gotten it down to a clear, comfortable presentation ask if you can give it at church. When you really are confident with telling your story it is time to look for opportunities to tell it wherever you go.

This is evangelism in its basic form and everyone should do it. Your story never gets old and when you tell it with honesty and genuine passion people will listen. Jesus told the demoniac to go and tell what great things the Lord had done. If he could do it so can you! As you go, be sensitive, honest and enthusiastic and you will be amazed how He can anoint your simplest words. If you embrace this truth and begin to apply it in your life you will touch many and bring some into the Kingdom of God. When you get right down to it, there is no simpler or more pure form of evangelism than this for believers.

In concluding this section on the gifts, I want the reader to take note that the gift ministries mentioned in Ephesians 4:11-12 are really the five core natures of God. These manifest depending on what He is doing in that season of your life. His apostolic nature comes when you need order and structure. His prophetic nature manifests when you need to hear His voice. His evangelistic nature shows up when relationship with Him and others is a priority. The pastoral nature will be strongest when you need care and protection. Finally, His teaching nature will be there when you need revelation and instruction. Whatever season you are in, recognize the nature of His presence during that time and you will benefit the most from it and be blessed.

* * * * * * * * * * *

**Go, tell what
great things the
Lord has done!**

* * * * * * * * * * *

IDENTIFYING FALSE PROPHECY

W hen speaking about false prophecy an important question must first be asked. Does a prophet speak a declaration of what is going to happen, or does a prophecy come to pass because a prophet spoke it? Scripture indicates that it is actually a combination of both. A prophet speaks out what God has revealed to them, but that act of speaking also sets things in motion from God's perspective, so it will come to pass. Once prophecy is released into the atmosphere things begin to happen, so you could say it is a divine partnership between the Lord, the prophet and the prophecy.

From the beginning it has been the voice of God that set all creation into motion. God did not wave His hand around or send a penetrating look to release His creativity. He simply spoke and it was so. Revelation 14:2 says His voice is like *"the sound of many waters,"* which in scientific terms is called "white noise." If you have ever heard huge ocean waves or been to Niagara Falls, you have heard this sound exploding out as the thunderous mass of water plunges over the edge of the falls. It causes a physical sensation to both the ears and to the body. You can actually feel it vibrating all through you. This is simply the energy of the *"voice of many waters"* being released.

Now take that and multiply it infinitely in both the natural and spirit realms and you begin to understand what God's voice is like. He thundered "LET THERE BE ..." and all of creation exploded into being. His voice actually rippled across time and space to create what was not yet in existence, and there it was. His magnificent voice created all that was not, into everything that we now know as the visible and the invisible realities of this life, and the one to come. That vibration was so massive that it still vibrates today in every atom that exists. Even at "absolute zero," the vibrational after shock of God's voice still causes every atom of all matter to vibrate at the sub atomic level. It never, ever stops!

So, when His voice is uttered, things have to happen. Thus, when He speaks through His prophets their voice aligns on earth with what is being spoken in heaven. In case you missed it that means the act of a prophet speaking actually sets things in motion. Isaiah 55:10-11 (NKJV) says;

"For as the rain comes down, and the snow from heaven, and do not return there, but water the earth, and make it bring forth and bud, that it may give seed to the sower and bread to the eater, so shall My word be that goes forth from My mouth; it shall not return to Me void, but it shall accomplish what I please, and it shall prosper in the thing for which I sent it."

A word that goes forth from His mouth can actually be released through the mouth of a prophet. When that word is spoken, it is fully released into its purpose and it is going to do the job it was sent to do.

The bread of creation moves from the mouth of God and gives life to the existence and destiny of man. This is why Deuteronomy 8:3 and Matthew 4:4 both declare that *"man does not live by bread alone, but by every word that proceeds from the mouth of God."*

The word "live" in Deut. 8:3 is a Hebrew word that means "to come to life, to be kept alive, to be healed and preserved." Thus, our destiny and our prophetic future is literally created, preserve and kept alive for us through that spoken word. Even though it was spoken by a human prophet, it was still Gods word, and it still brings to bear God's creative authority to speak all things into existence.

Notice how it says this in 1 Samuel 3:19-21;(NKJV)

> *"So Samuel grew, and the Lord was with him and let none of his words fall to the ground. And all Israel from Dan to Beersheba knew that Samuel had been established as a prophet of the Lord. Then the Lord appeared again in Shiloh. For the Lord revealed Himself to Samuel in Shiloh by the word of the Lord."*

It is interesting to note that it says God let none of Samuels words fall to the ground. It does not say that God let none of His own words fall to the ground. What Samuel spoke actually became the creative tool God used to shape the existence and destiny of the nation. It was a perfect partnership. As the prophet heard God and spoke, God backed up what he said. Not only that, this scripture says God actually used those creative words to reveal Himself to Samuel. Samuel's word became both a creator of national destiny and a literal revelation of the One who designed it. Don't miss that powerful point because it is a key to identifying true prophecy. The genuine nature of God is always revealed in genuine prophecy.

This same powerful truth is found in 2 Kings 10:10. God desired to bring His judgment against the house of Ahab for what he and Jezebel had done. How did He do it? He did it through the spoken words of Elijah. Here we read:

> *"Know now that nothing shall fall to the earth of the word of*
> *the Lord which the Lord spoke concerning the house of Ahab;*
> *for the Lord has done what He spoke by His servant Elijah."*

Take special note of the order in which things happened. God first spoke to the heart of Elijah. Next Elijah personally speaks audibility to Ahab. Once that word was released on the earth it would not rest until it revealed God's righteousness and accomplished the purpose for which it had been sent. No wonder the writer of Hebrews said;

> *For the word of God is living and powerful, and sharper*
> *than any two-edged sword, piercing even to the division*
> *of soul and spirit, and of joints and marrow, and is a*
> *discerner of the thoughts and intents of the heart.*
> HEBREWS 4:12 NKJV

Once a prophet hears from God and speaks His word out into the atmosphere, things begin to happen. The creative life of God is a living, active and powerful truth that begins to create a new reality. It will cut through every life circumstance, divide the natural from the spiritual, and reveal the condition of every heart in order to reveal God and align everything for His purposes. All of this happens just because a genuine prophet speaks.

This also explains why it is so important for a prophet to guard their lips and carefully choose their words. They must always speak that which releases the life of God into a situation. If they are creating realities by what they say, then their words must reflect who God is. To not do so is contrary to the purpose of their ministry and it brings them into a place of serious accountability before the Lord.

How False Prophecy Happens

Since New Testament prophets are the mind, heart and mouthpiece of the Lord to His people. What they speak truly can be from God, but what is said must be evaluated and judged for content, accuracy, style of delivery, timing, consistency, spiritual life and heart attitude. Every valid prophetic utterance will have the "Logos" or life of God in it, and will have Gods heart attitude woven through it. If it has these core elements then it should be considered a true word from the Lord, and can be fully embraced.

I have been asked on several occasions how false prophecy happens. In some cases false prophecy has its source in the prophets natural mind or natural powers of observation. This most often occurs when prophets speak from their own thoughts because of visual cues. In other words, they see something with the natural eye and their thoughts make it into a word from the Lord. That is, they see a person limping and then have a "word" from the Lord that the person is in pain or needs healing. I have observed this many times and sadly, most people still don't see it for what it is.

However, false prophecy is not just a matter of saying the wrong thing. It is more frequently a matter of speaking with a wrong heart attitude, wrong timing or wrong style of delivery. It is often given by someone who is a genuine prophet but has a fleshly, carnal or emotionally messed up life. Unresolved personal issues always pollute a prophetic word. These things act like filters that defile the content and spirit of what God intends to say. In essence these are the main elements of false prophecy. They must be carefully considered when a prophetic word is spoken or going to be believed. In other words, do you really know and trust the emotional and spiritual life of the one speaking?

False prophecy is not something to be taken lightly. I have known many people in the last few moves of God who have been told that false prophecy, also called "missing it," is just a harmless mistake made by flawed humans. They believe it's no big deal and nothing to get concerned about. Many have been taught that anyone can and should open their mouth and give a "thus says the Lord." They believe that God understands when we miss it and there's no harm done. Since we are now under grace it's nothing to be concerned about. This is not only unscriptural but it presents something very dangerous that must be considered.

False prophecy is not to be taken lightly.

It's true that God does understand when we miss it. However, that doesn't mean He condones, approves or excuses it away. Most of all it certainly does not mean there is no harm done. I was told the following by one over-zealous woman who bounced in and out of our church. She received some kind of prophetic "training" at a prophecy conference and was instructed: "Don't make such a big deal out of it. We can all prophesy. Just open your mouth and let it rip!"

When corrected, she left our church with a defiant attitude and went on to speak "words" over many people she met. Her spiritual six guns were blazing! In a very short time she brought great confusion, destruction and trouble into the lives of everyone who listened to her. They became as unteachable and unstable as she was once they foolishly believed the "words" she had spoken over them. The real tragedy is that this kind of illegitimate ministry discredits the real thing, and it always wounds the innocent.

When prophecy is only built around training and experimental use of the gift, things are going to get strange. If there is no regard given to the consequences of these words, many are going to get wounded and hurt. All too often, someone's zeal to use a newly activated gift is nothing more than a showcase for their own striving for recognition and inflated ego. Unfortunately, this presents a grave danger to those who innocently receive words from such unbalanced and untested sources.

The danger of believing and following a missed word is graphically portrayed in Jer. 28:10-13. As you read the Scripture below keep in mind what happened when the people followed the missed word.

> *"Then Hananiah the prophet took the yoke from the neck of Jeremiah the prophet and broke it. And Hananiah spoke in the presence of all the people, saying, "Thus says the LORD, 'Even so will I break within two full years, the yoke of Nebuchadnezzar king of Babylon from the neck of all the nations.'" Then the prophet Jeremiah went his way. And the word of the LORD came to Jeremiah, after Hananiah the prophet had broken the yoke from off the neck of the prophet Jeremiah, saying, "Go and speak to Hananiah, saying, 'Thus says the LORD, "You have broken the yokes of wood, but you have made instead of them yokes of iron."*

When Hananiah spoke and made others believe he was hearing from God, it set in motion a false belief in the hearts of those who heard it. They were already confused and uncertain about what to do. This word propelled them even further in the wrong direction. Rather than believing what God was really saying, they believed and acted upon what was wrong, and this made their situation much worse. This missed word pointed them in a direction God was not going, and that misdirection hurt them more than they could have possibly imagined.

Hananiah's word brought upon the people a yoke of iron in exchange for what had been a yolk of wood. God would now deal more severely with them because the false word had sent them in a false direction. What seemed so good actually made their situation worse. It was not some harmless mistake. The fact is, that word changed their lives and caused them great trouble. It's easy to see that a missed word is never some harmless mistake to be fluffed off and overlooked. It can have far-reaching, even deadly consequences for the one who embraces it and acts upon it.

Parking Lot Problem

An example of this almost happened in our church in the summer of 2005. Prophet Kim Clement was to minister at a church in Albany, NY. However, he was held up at the airport and never could do the meeting. As a result many people arrived at the host church only to find the meeting had been canceled. Emotions ran high and a prophetic atmosphere was present simply because the people were fired up with expectation. Unfortunately, many decided they would hang around and have their own, unsupervised prophetic meeting in the church parking lot.

Kim's bass player, Charlie Jordan, is a good friend of ours, and when we saw him we brought him home with us. As we left, what was happening all over the parking lot sent a shiver of concern up my spine. Against all biblical standards, there were parking lot prophecies flying in all directions. Words were pouring out of everyone's mouth to anything that was breathing. We addressed our apprehension to a few who were standing nearby and then headed for home.

To our shock and disbelief, we learned the next day that an unknown person had in fact spoken over a young man and a young lady from our congregation. They had arrived late for the meeting and were unknowingly caught in the prophetic sewer that was flowing. The young man had been told he would be president of the United States while the young girl was told she was now anointed as an evangelist to her elementary school.

When the information got back to us I quickly called the parents of those young people and began to ask some very important questions. The answers I got back were not good, and far from what I expected. After sharing Scripture, I was able to convince the parents to release these heavy, unbalanced and potentially destructive words off their children. In addition I instructed the parents about the danger they had placed their whole family in by swimming in such a spiritual cesspool.

This incident taught Esther and I a very important lesson. Even when good teaching has been done, solid people can still be caught up and swept away in the moment. They can be moved by the wrong spiritual fire and quickly place themselves in danger. Things can look innocent enough, but if the source is wrong it can bring a massive set of problems down the road.

Even solid people can be caught up and swept away in the moment.

Why is parking lot prophecy so dangerous? The answer is quite simple. First of all, through experience I know that 99% of them are wrong, and the 1% that may be correct, still are not right. Why is that? Because the person who gave it did not honor the lines of pastoral authority in the person's life! They spoke into someone's life when their God-appointed leadership was not present. This is the reason Psalms 16:6 is so important. It says, *"The lines have fallen to me in pleasant places; Indeed, my heritage is beautiful to me."*

Your spiritual heritage is literally found within, and defined by where the lines of authority fall in your life. When you allow anyone to speak into your destiny, they insert their influence and authority in your life stream. By so doing, they have not honored the lines of authority God placed there, and you are in danger of trading away your spiritual inheritance by listening to, and foolishly following the authority and voice of another.

You may be thinking right now "Why is this so?" The answer is relatively simple. If a false word is embraced, God has to begin dealing in new ways in the life of the one who embraced it. As the person moves further and further away from where they should actually be going, God must bring them back into the fire and back into the furnace to purge away the dross that the false word put in them. Back on the potter's wheel they go in order to return them to the center of what God planned for their life. Had they not received that word in the first place, none of this would be necessary.

In the case of Hananiah, his word brought more trouble on the people than what they started with. He was wrong, but the people believed it. Because of this, they traded a yoke of wood for what became a much heavier, and more difficult yoke of iron. In the case of the young people I mentioned, the burden of such a word was way beyond their years, even if by some miracle it might have been true. It was a crushing burden that no child should have to carry. Such words would have pushed them in a direction at a time God never intended. Nothing could be more destructive to a young, impressionable life. With God, timing is everything. The only thing more frustrating than being out of the will of God is being out of His timing, and the devil knows it.

This is the great danger of speaking as if it is God when it's not. It causes people to believe and do the wrong thing. They head in the wrong direction and this always brings confusion. They expend time, energy and resources to accomplish something that God never designed, and will not bless. In the end, people become discouraged and even bitter at God when a false word fails to come to pass. What's even worse, the person's true calling in life will be delayed and in some cases, even lost.

False prophecy is not a harmless activity.

Giving a false prophecy is not some harmless mistake. It can be quite deadly and people who flippantly release such words practice spiritual malpractice of the worst kind. They are playing spiritual Russian roulette with the soul, the life and the destiny of God's people. Eventually there will come a day of great responsibility for the pain, misdirection and lost ministry that these people, and their "words," have caused. If you have given such words, or been on the receiving end one, now is the time to take a moment in prayer to repent and get that straightened out with the Lord.

When There Is No Anointing

There is another thing to consider when a prophetic word spoken over your life is actually incorrect. It's not just some harmless miss that you can blow off. The demonic forces assigned to you only know what they hear. That means they have no idea if a word you are given is incorrect. As a result, they begin to target you and plot your downfall as if you were actually anointed for, and called to manifest that word. You must understand that this becomes a double hit in your life and ministry.

This is because you are now going to be worked on and attacked by demonic forces for something you were never called or anointed to fulfill. This brings problems into your life that should not have been there in the first place. Isaiah 10:27 makes it very clear that the anointing in your life is what breaks every yoke. When you are attacked for something you are not anointed to do, there is no protection. That means the yoke of bondage the enemy throws at you in order to hinder a ministry you don't actually have, will not be easily broken. You are stuck battling something that was never supposed to be your fight.

So, not only are you continually subjected to unwarranted attacks, you are especially vulnerable to those attacks because there is no anointing to protect a ministry that does not exist in your life. Needless to say, this is never a good place to be in. This is also why receiving prophetic ministry from just anyone who comes along can become a very spiritually dangerous and emotionally frustrating thing. The bottom line is, avoid this all together by not letting it happen to you.

There is another area I want to address as well when it comes to the reality of false prophecy. This is the concept of a word being technically correct but it has been delivered with a wrong heart, wrong attitude or at the wrong time. In addition it can be delivered in such an unclear way that it does not accurately represent the heart of God. Words of this nature do not have the "Logos" or life of God in them, and this is the key element behind the following;

> *"Moreover, He said to me, "Son of man, take into your heart*
> *all My words which I shall speak to you, and listen closely."*
> EZEK.3:10

The truth behind the above Scripture is powerful. It explains why a word can be technically accurate but still be a false prophecy. This happens because the prophet who delivered it did not take the word of God into his heart. He heard what God said, but did not feel what God felt when He said it. The prophet simply got information from the knowledge of God in the spirit realm but he did not get revelation from the heart of God. In case you missed my point, this is a huge problem. That's because only revelation from God's heart, not information from God's head, is what causes a word to be filled with God's life.

When prophets operate from their gifting, and get the mind of God without getting His heart, the word will be technically correct but it will not contain His nature. If this happens, what is released is not a reflection of the will of the Lord, nor does it demonstrate His real character. Words of this type may be verbally correct, but they are still not true. Seeds of confusion always get released into those who receive such words. Hang onto these thoughts and in the next chapter we will take a much closer look at how all this fits together.

When it comes to a false authority speaking a false word into your life, don't allow it. If you do and embrace what was said, you have given demonic forces an open door to mess with your destiny. The devil will come after you for something you are not called to do, and since you have no anointing to break off his yoke, deliverance from it will be slow in coming. Since you are not equipped to deal with it, you are going to have seasons of unnecessary trouble that could have been avoided. If people really understood this principle, they could easily prevent bringing such trouble upon themselves.

With this knowledge firmly in hand, you are now ready to move to the next aspect of what it means to speak a genuine prophetic word. In the chapter that follows we will take an in depth look at the power of prophesy, and how it can influence people on many different levels. We will also see why it is so important to know who is speaking into your life, and why this can either help or hinder your walk in God. These essentials will build a solid foundation for you to properly answer your call to any level of the prophetic.

The Two Kinds Of Prophecy

Let me end this chapter by identifying the two kinds of prophecy found in Scripture. This will clear up some of the misunderstandings people have about the concept of false prophecy and false prophets. The first kind of prophecy is God's **prophetic plan**. The second kind is God's **prophetic will,** and this is very different.

Prophecy which falls under God's plan is an absolute. It is an immutable prophetic word fixed in the mind of God and it is going to happen. It is something He has purposed by His own design for a specific reason and season. History flows to and through these prophetic words and mankind has no bearing on their manifestation or outcome. God has within His own mind a specific purpose for this event to happen at the appointed prophetic time.

Israel leaving Egypt for the Promised Land in Exodus 3, the 70 years of Jewish captivity in Jeremiah 25, the birth of the Messiah in Isaiah 7, and the abomination of desolation Jesus spoke of in Matthew 24:15 are just a few examples of the above. Each was prophesied as God's prophetic plan within human history, and each happens at the fullness of prophetic time for the purpose God intends. These are markers, or signposts that human history will flow around and nothing man does can stop these divine decrees from manifesting where and when their time has come.

All other prophecy falls under God's prophetic will. His prophetic will is prophesied to people and places but it is influenced and impacted by the actions of men. The prophetic will of God requires us to cooperate with it in order for it to happen. Keep in mind that His prophetic will fits under the umbrella of His prophetic plan, and that's important to know. Even though people may be part of God's plan, they will never see His will unfolded for them unless they do what is required for it to manifest.

The prophetic will of God requires our cooperation.

A clear example of this is found in Exodus 3 when Moses is told God's prophetic plan that Israel will go to the Promised Land. Moses is also told God's prophetic will that he is God's prophet to speak the word of the Lord to Israel and lead them into the Promised Land. Unfortunately, when you examine Scripture you find out something transpired that is quite disturbing. You discover that the plan of God did happen, but the will of God did not! After 40 years in the wilderness the nation entered the Promised Land, just as Moses had said. However, Moses and that whole generation died along the way. As a genuine prophet of God, Moses proclaimed God's word to Israel, yet it never happened. How do you reconcile that? According to some teachings this would have to mean that Moses was a false prophet.

Those who don't understand the difference between the two kinds of prophecy will have a massive issue right now! Consider what Jesus said in Matthew 18:14: *"It is the will of the Father that none should perish,"* yet we know that people die and go to hell every day. Jesus declared the Father's will, yet we know there are many cases where it does not come to pass. So, does that make Jesus false? When you understand God's prophetic plan verses Gods prophetic will, you can reconcile these prophetic realities. The plan of God is a done deal that is set in place by the Father. The will of God is a divine possibility that is subject to our cooperation.

This will help you define who is, and who is not, a false prophet. Don't start calling someone false simply because the word they gave you did not come to pass. Scripture says, *"Many are called but few are chosen."* Why? Because the call, God's prophetic will, only identifies what His design is for your life. That same call comes with specific requirements you must meet. If you receive a word but refuse to change, will not mature and keep doing your own thing, you have voided that prophecy. Don't blame the prophet when it was your own irresponsibility and stubborn resistance to authority that killed your prophetic word. Once you uncover this truth it changes everything and the pieces fit.

A word that
is technically
correct can still
be delivered
with a wrong
heart, wrong
attitude, or at
the wrong time.

THE POWER OF A PROPHETIC WORD

Understand that every prophetic word has a life of it's own. It is imparted through and connected to God's life, and the life that is in the one who delivers it. If the messenger is messed up, if they have no character development and don't have the heart of God, then the word they release will be a polluted, messed up mixture as well. There is no choice in this matter. A prophet can only give to others what is actually living in them. What they have is all they can give away. This means that the ability to accurately prophesy is not what makes a prophet reliable.

Another thing to consider is the timing of a word. By not knowing the timing of God for the release of a prophetic word, a huge problem can be set in motion in someone's life. A true word that is released prematurely will frustrate the one it is intended for in many ways. Not only will they be unprepared to receive it, they will also be unequipped to walk in it successfully. Moving on a premature word, even if it is valid, will cause more difficulty than can be imagined in someone's life.

One issue of great importance is in knowing that the prophet delivering the word has both permission and authority to release it. They must be fully operating in their metron for this to be in biblical order. Prophets do not have universal permission to operate every place they go, or to speak into the lives of everyone they meet. As was already stated, they must respect the lines of authority God has set in place, and submit under the pastoral oversight of those they minister to. God gives His sheep to specific shepherds, and those shepherds are responsible to lead and feed the sheep under their charge.

I experienced a clear example of this truth in 1999. A respected educator I had never met before was brought to my church with the hope of receiving a prophetic word. He and I had a mutual friend who asked me to minister to him after our Sunday morning service. I laid my hands on him and received a clear word for his life and future. Before speaking I asked him if his pastor was present. When he said "no" I then asked if he had permission from his pastor to receive the word God had given me. Again he said "no".

At this point I informed him I could not give him the prophetic word. I explained that a genuine prophet is required to respect pastoral authority. Since his pastor was not present I did not have the right or the authority to sow prophetic seed into his life. He was puzzled by this, but then the Lord released me to say; "In two weeks, another prophet will call you out. That prophet will give you this word of the Lord when your pastor is present".

I forgot all about that brief encounter until I met the man again one evening in August of 2006. My wife and I had been invited to minister prophetically in a cell group established under Mt. Zion Ministries of Utica, NY (now Redeemer Church) and this same man happened to be attending the cell group that night. What he told me confirmed that God does indeed honor those who respect lines of authority.

He said that after I had spoken over him he left somewhat perplexed. However, exactly two weeks to the very hour, he actually received the prophecy I had spoken about. Prophetess Cindy Jacobs pointed him out of a crowd of 1200 people. With his pastor present she delivered the prophetic word God had promised him. Through this incident it was made clear to me just how important it is to honor the "lines" God has set in someone's life. When a prophet does not respect those lines of authority do not allow them to speak into your life. If you do you may end up getting something more than you bargained for.

Another problem area comes through prophets who have a rebellious, unteachable or legalistic spirit. Others may be struggling with emotional wounds, a spirit of offence, a spirit of rejection or some kind of emotional instability. As a result, **The mess is** they will release words that end up causing **delivered** damage since these personal issues will filter how **with the** they hear God, and how they speak for Him. **message.** Each issue can influence what is heard, and how it is finally released. Never forget that emotional problems and unhealthy character traits that are unresolved always pose a problem in the life and ministry of any five-fold minister.

It is very true that our mess does indeed become our message. As God deals with us, He finally makes the changes within that we need in order to successfully walk out our life ministry. This is a good thing. However, when that mess has not been transformed into a clear life message, that's not good. Every prophet who really wants to impact lives for the better, must seek God for their own personal transformation first. With that transformation comes the qualification necessary to sow pure, 100 fold prophetic "seed" into the lives of those who listen.

The fact is, every internal issue that remains unhealed will influence our reception from God, our relationship with others and our delivery of what He says. There is no way to avoid the mixed impartation that comes from a prophet who is in emotional turmoil, or who has an unrefined character. The mess inside the prophet is going to be imparted a piece at a time with every message they deliver.

Mixed seed always produces a defiled, messed up crop.

In reality this is just like throwing mixed seed into the fertile soil of someone's heart. According to God's word mixed seed always produces a defiled, messed up crop. The end result is that the individual, or even the church that embraced the word, will be worse off. It would have been better not to have received the word in the first place, and this is the principle behind Deuteronomy 22:9. Here we read:

"...You shall not sow your vineyard with two kinds of seed, lest all the produce of the seed which you have sown, and the increase of the vineyard become defiled."

Mixture produces confusion, and everything that confusion touches becomes defiled. That is also why James 1:8 and James 4:8 say:

"a double-minded man is unstable in all his ways" and the double- minded must *"...purify their heart..."*

It is also why 1 Kings 18:21 adds:

"How long will you hesitate between two opinions? If the LORD is God, follow Him; but if Baal, follow him." But the people did not answer him a word."

Whenever there are unhealthy things deposited along with a prophetic word, these will eventually manifest and paralyze the recipient from moving on. It will take away their focus, bring frustration and eventually misdirect them in a number of different ways. In the end such words carry the deadly ability to choke out all the seed that really is good within the person.

I learned a very hard lesson on this early in my ministry. I was a young prophet and receiving calls to travel to many churches. Year after year I went and released clear, detailed words to people and the pastors knew I was "spot on". However, after a few years of going to the same churches I felt troubled in the Lord. It was clear that there was no lasting change or real deposit of God's life being left behind in the churches where I spoke.

What the Lord finally showed me was painful but true. The issues in me I would not deal with were being imparted, reproduced in, and manifested through those I had ministered to. Prophetically I would help them in one area only to place in them the impatience, need for recognition and insecurity that was still living in me. With this revelation things began to change for me. Over time I allowed God to do what had to be done within my heart and the results eventually showed up in the churches and the people I prophesied over.

This, more than any other thing, is the real reason for being so careful about who speaks over your life. When prophets impart what is good into good soil, good things will spring up. However, when prophets sow mixed seed into good soil, a mixed spiritual mess will thrive and that will produce an unwanted and unexpected harvest.

The Impact Of Prophecy

There is a massive impact on the heart, mind and spirit of the one who receives a prophetic word. Once that word is delivered, be it good or bad, it goes down into the inner core of the person and makes changes in how they think, what they believe and what they begin to move towards. If the word spoken is not right, it's impact will not be right either. The influence of double mindedness, emotional instability, bitterness, anger, lust or a host of other things will poison the delivery of a genuine prophetic word every time.

Thus, great damage comes from the one who may have a remarkable gift but has a clear lack of character development or emotional stability. In light of this, Proverbs 13:17 takes on new meaning when it says, *"A wicked messenger falls into adversity, But a faithful envoy brings healing."*

As a messenger of God, every prophet must know their heart is clean, their character is well developed and their attitude is properly aligned with God. In addition their motives must also be pure and right. If these things are not in order they will release an impure word every time, which brings instability, confusion and distraction to those they minister to. According to Proverbs 13:17, not only will they fall into adversity but so will those who receive the word.

Proverbs 18:21 says that *"death and life are in the power of the tongue and those who love it will eat it's fruit."* What comes out of my mouth as a prophet will either benefit or hurt the hearer. If I come like a "faithful envoy" what I bring with me will produce life, health and healing. If my character is bad or my motives are not pure, I will release something very different.

The Ten Tests Of Prophecy

False prophets and false prophecy in the New Testament are easy to identify. Below are ten tests that can be used to recognize the false from the true. Any word you give or receive that does not line up with this standard should be rejected no matter how good it sounds.

The Test Of:

1. **Heart** - Is it ministered with God's heart? (Matt 7:22-23)

2. **Character** - Does the one who delivered it have emotional stability and good character? (Matt 12:36-37)

3. **Life** - Is God's life/logos in it and is He the source of it? (John 8:11)

4. **Clarity** - Is it delivered in a clear, understandable way? (1 Cor. 14:8-9, 31-33)

5. **Timing** - Is it the right time for the word to be delivered? (Eccl 3:1)

6. **Authority** - Is the one who delivered it under authority and are they in their "metron"? (2 Cor. 10:12-13)

7. **Alignment** – Does it line up with other valid words you have received from recognized, seasoned prophets? (1 kings 13:16-24)

8. **Scripture** - Does it contradict Scripture in any way? (Is 8:20)

9. **Fulfillment** - Does it come to pass? (1 kings 13:32)

10. **Witness** – Does it bear witness with the Spirit of God in you and with your leadership? (John 15:26)

If every aspect of prophetic ministry were examined in the light of these 10 tests, there would be a much greater love, respect and acceptance of prophets and prophetic ministry in the church today. People would find that there is a great benefit from knowing how to properly understand, walk in and fight for the things God has spoken over their life.

Since churches either tend to reject prophetic ministry all together, or embrace everything that comes along, there is little balance to be found. It is only through the power of seasoned prophets that we can unlock this ministry and release it back to the church, and the marketplace. May God give us the wisdom to see this much-needed ministry restored to the place of influence, authority and honor that it once had.

Every prophet
must know
their heart is
clean, their
character is well
developed and
their attitude is
properly aligned
with God.

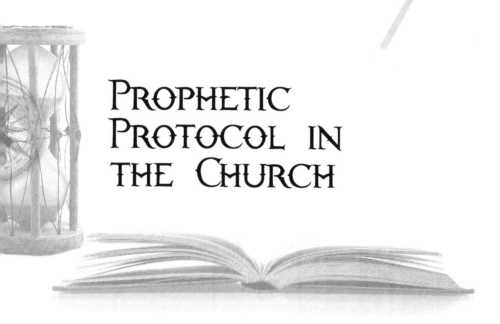

PROPHETIC PROTOCOL IN THE CHURCH

There is a God-ordained order for how prophets are to function in the Body of Christ in general, and in the local church. Paul addressed this critical issue in 1 Cor. 14:29-33, and verses 37-38. In these passages he set the gold standard for all prophets to follow. Here we read;

> *"And let two or three prophets speak, and let the others*
> *(other prophets) pass judgment. But if a revelation is made*
> *to another (prophet) who is seated, let the first (prophet) keep*
> *silent. For you (all the prophets) can all prophesy one by one,*
> *so that all may learn and all may be exhorted; and the spirits*
> *of prophets are subject to prophets; for God is not a God of*
> *confusion but of peace, as in all the churches of the Saints."*
> *(Words in parenthesis added by the author to clarify.)*
> *"If anyone thinks he is a prophet or spiritual, let him recognize*
> *that the things which I write to you are the Lord's commandment.*
> *But if anyone does not recognize this, he is not recognized."*

The Scriptures above clearly establish a prophetic protocol that should be known and followed by prophets. As you read this over please consider carefully what the Scriptures are really establishing. These are not laws or rules that have been chipped in stone. They are principles that provide a spiritual and practical structure to bring order to prophetic ministry. These things keep a spirit of honor flowing between those who are prophets and the other leaders in the church. Since God saw fit to include these clear instructions in such a prominent way, we cannot afford to ignore or marginalize them.

First of all it says in verse 29 that prophets are to judge each other as they deliver prophetic words. Because of the level of insight and revelation that prophets operate in, only another prophet will recognize some elements of the ministry that may be off. To put it another way, most people can't go into a local hospital and sit down to judge the work of a brain surgeon. Why? One must be called to and trained in that level of the medical profession to judge what is going on. Aside from recognizing a major blunder where a patient dies or is crippled, most people would have no clue as to what was correct procedure when it came to evaluating such a high level of surgical skill. Thus, it takes a genuine prophet, who flows in the same prophetic office, to accurately judge the ministry of another prophet.

Prophets Correct Prophets

An example of this happened to my wife and I not long ago. We were asked to be part of a prophetic presbytery team at the opening of a new church. The other prophet on our team was well respected and we really enjoyed working with him that evening. He had a clear word and a proven ministry.

During the ministry time he began to minister a word over two couples who were called to be in the leadership of that new church. As I listened to the word, I realized what he said was off a bit regarding the ministry of each couple. Since I had never worked with this brother before I simply waited until he was done and then stepped in to speak the specific ministries that each of the four were called to. The adjustment was done with grace and with such care that no one recognized it for what it was.

The next day I contacted the pastor and the overseeing apostle of the church to make sure they had picked up what I had done. They had actually missed it but were glad I had not. I then explained how the other word was slightly off and they agree. I did this because I wanted to be sure that the error would be made clear to the two couples. Had we not made this slight adjustment those so new in their ministry could have begun to move in the wrong direction, and that would not have been good. No one but another prophet could have picked up what I did, and that is why it is so important for prophets to cover and correct one another.

This is exactly why it's so important to understand that it takes another prophet to evaluate the ministry of a prophet. Only a prophet will have the insight necessary to recognize and judge the specific elements of another prophet's ministry. Some aspects can be judged by anyone, but one who is not a prophet cannot understand the timing of the word or the nature of it when it is personal or directive for the future. Such things as a call to a mission field or a future call to five-fold ministry would be examples of this. Only another prophet would recognize and accurately judge the validity of this higher prophetic order.

An example of this happened when I was very young in Christ, and I was called forward to receive prophetic presbytery. As they spoke over me the younger prophet said I was an elder in the church. Immediately the more seasoned prophets stepped up and said, "No, he is an elder in the making." That adjustment was definitely needed and it saved my church all the problems that would have come by too quickly promoting me.

The Scriptures make it clear that it is the responsibility of prophets to provide the needed spiritual insight, balance and correction for each other. By doing so, they guard the ministry and protect the sheep from words that have missed the mark in one-way or another. By submitting under authority, and being open to correction and adjustment one prophet can keep the ministry of another in proper alignment.

Secondly, prophets who work as a team are to give place to one another and not act as a one-man show. Because of the office they hold, they are like a conduit and each has the potential to just keep flowing, going and releasing the word of the Lord. Since prophets can release what God gives them in a continual flow, they must be sensitive to one another and willing to stay silent when God gives a revelation to another *"who is seated."*

Seasoned prophets show honor, they have no need to compete.

By operating this way, not only do they show honor for one another, but more importantly, a much fuller prophetic word is released as each prophet gives their part of the revelation. When prophets speak one by one, the parts fit together like the pieces of a puzzle. A much clearer prophetic blueprint emerges over those receiving ministry when prophets operate as a unified team. Eccl 7:27 puts it this way:

> *"Behold, I have discovered this," says the Preacher, "adding one thing to another to find an explanation,"*

Thirdly, how a prophet delivers a word is subject to his own character and human spirit. 1 Cor. 14:32 speaks clearly about the prophet's human spirit and personal character traits. *Here it says; "and the spirits of prophets are subject to prophets."* It's clear that in context, this passage does not refer to the Holy Spirit, as some have taught. Scripture never says we become mindless robots in the hand of an all-powerful God. There is no indicator that He over-rules our personality or personal traits and habits to accomplish His will. God's influence upon us may be recognizable, but we are still who we are as we deliver any prophetic word.

My experience with young prophets and Christians in general, is that they imitate what they have seen. If they watch someone take a certain stance or act a certain way when God used them, they tend to imitate that behavior. To the untrained or the inexperienced, such things appear to be "spiritual." Prophets who feel they must act "other worldly" or they get "King Jamesites" (speak in King James English when they prophesy) do themselves and their ministry a great disservice.

No place in Scripture is strange or odd behavior necessary, or considered spiritual. However, it can be religious, distracting and quite detrimental to the prophet's ministry. Since these things can actually prevent the reception of the word of the Lord, I strongly suggest that prophets avoid them all together. King James English is not wrong, it's just not necessary. Most of all it does not validate a word if it's not from God. It is always best to just be yourself, and allow God to use you exactly the way He made you.

Another thing happened not long ago when my wife and I were asked to be part of an installation service for a new church. We were teamed up with another prophet we had never worked with before. He was highly respected by this church and it was clear to us that his heart was tender towards God. However, as we began to minster he apparently had been in a meeting where blowing on the people was the thing to do.

As I began to prophesy over those being installed, this man started blowing in my direction. Not only was this very distracting, but he had apparently eaten garlic that day and the smell was almost nauseating. We were able to finish the meeting with grace but it posed a problem that I had to work through. Needless to say, if that were to ever happen again I would take the liberty to stop it. Such actions can be fine if they are directed by the Spirit, but when they are not, they add noting but confusion.

Our Nature

Every prophet must remember that God does not over-rule their nature. This is clearly evidenced in the life of Moses when he had his encounter at the burning bush. In Exodus 4 we see something happen that points this very thing out. Moses knew he did not speak well and began to argue with God. God then tells him something quite interesting. He says:

> *"... Who has made man's mouth? Or who makes him dumb or deaf, or seeing or blind? Is it not I, the LORD? {12} "Now then go, and I, even I, will be with your mouth, and teach you what you are to say."*
>
> *EX. 4:11-12 NASB*

Notice that God says He will teach him what he is to say. In other words, it will be a learning process for Moses. He does not go through some instantaneous transformation to make him somehow more spiritual or better qualified. God makes it clear that Moses can learn a new way to speak but he must yield that weakness to the Lord. God will not take control of him, over-rule his personality, or circumvent his personal weaknesses to make him become something he is not. He used him just as he was, and we must never forget that God does the same with us.

Moses had to become bolder in some cases, even thought he was given the ability to demonstrate the miraculous powers of God. However, in the end it was still God using Moses as a weak, flawed man. The man was doing it, just the way he was. In spite of all his frailty and inconsistencies, it was still Moses. In this way it was clear that God would get the honor and glory, and it had little to do with the ability of the man He was using.

How does this translate into prophets and their prophetic ministry today? The answer is so obvious that until now everyone has missed it.

Even under God's power, and when speaking God's word, a prophet is still who they are. For the most part they don't become some strange acting, hyper-spiritual, totally different person. In some cases I have seen the Lord over-ride something that may be a hindrance to the release of the ministry, such as stuttering, but the person was still who they were.

Why is that important to know? If a prophet is verbose, disjointed and unfocused in life, these tendencies will often show up in their prophetic ministry as well. If they tend to become sidetracked and never get to the point, the clarity and power of any prophecy they deliver will also be lost in a multitude of unimportant details. If they are blunt, abrasive, abrupt or harsh with people on a daily basis, they will also tend to be that way in their prophetic ministry. The fact is, God does not overtake our natural tendencies, and we do not become controlled contrary to the nature that is ruling us. We are who we are and that may need to be refined.

When you prophesy, you are who you are.

This is why God's Word indicates that bad habits, poorly developed character traits and unrestrained natural tendencies are harmful to a prophet's ministry. Because of this, every prophet must seek to develop their character, and work on how they deliver what God gives them. The unruly personal traits, bad habits and irritating characteristics they have in normal life will end up destroying the credibility of what they do in the spirit. Unless prophets mature and become well balanced as individuals, they will eventually stop people from receiving their ministry, even if it truly is from the Lord.

Who Prophets Are And What They Do

Prophets function in their ministry based upon who they are. This in part, is due to the gifts that reside within them. Beyond that they literally are the gift of Jesus to His church. The capacity to hear in the Spirit and move in that arena flows through them all the time. Each prophet may function at a different level and in a different way, but the capacity to operate in the Spirit and release their ministry is there because it is what God made them to do. It is their in-built design and automatically flows out of them.

Since this is their place in the Body of Christ, a prophet's ministry is based upon how God made them to function, not on the occasional operation of a spiritual gift. For this reason it is very important for prophets to have a rich prayer life and a deep intimate relationship with God. This is why I stress once again that these things, coupled with emotional maturity, good character development, mental stability and submission under apostolic authority are the foundation stones of a world-class ministry. If someone has an unrefined nature contrary to the above, it also means they will have a lesser place of trust and authority in God's Kingdom.

Releasing Prophetic Ministry

In early Pentecostal circles it was believed that one had to have a special feeling or be "moved" by the Spirit on some occasion in order to release a prophetic word. However, ministers like Smith Wigglesworth, Jack Coe, Oral Roberts, Kenneth Hagin and Bill Hamon were spiritual pioneers who broke from this incorrect theology. They discovered that they could move in the Holy Spirit by faith even if they did not feel the Holy Spirit moving in them.

In like fashion, the nature, flow and magnitude of what God shows a prophet gives them the potential to prophesy over anyone at any time. However, mature prophets will never do so, nor will they speak all that God shows them when they do prophesy. Seasoned prophets know they are not dependent on some momentary rush of the Holy Spirit that compels them to prophesy. They know their office, place in God and ministry is like a river that gushes forth continually. However, they also know they are to release that prophetic flow only as God directs.

Immature prophets, or those who occasionally operate in one of the vocal gifts, are prone to do what I call "grab and blab." What I mean is, the moment they grab something out of the Spirit, they feel compelled to blab it. Mature ministry, however, does not operate this way. Solid prophets only speak what God instructs them to, at the time He says to and to whom it is intended. They wait until they have His heart and then release what He gave them with great sensitivity. Any revelation given by the Holy Spirit is a great treasure and it must be handled with the utmost care. When things are out of synch, it can be devastating to the one being ministered to and the ministry of the prophet.

I learned the importance of this several years ago when I ministered prophetically over a husband and wife in Colebrook, New Hampshire. I did not know it at the time, but they had lost a son a few months earlier in a tragic accident. The child was suddenly killed by an 18-wheeler when he slipped from his father's hand and ran out into the road. The event devastated the truck driver, the entire family and the community in which they lived. It was so overwhelming that the father, mother and truck driver all ended up in the hospital from the emotional trauma they had suffered.

I knew nothing of the above information as the couple came forward to receive personal prophetic ministry. As they approached the front of the church prophet Steve Fedele pushed me in front of them to minister first, because he knew them and their situation. The closer they got the more I could feel great waves of grief, pain, sorrow and a deep sense of terrible, sudden loss in my spirit. As I laid my hands on them all the people in the church fell silent waiting to hear what God would say.

I began to prophesy over them about the compassion and broken heart of God for them. Then I saw in the Spirit that something had been instantaneously taken from them in an unexpected, terrifying accident and it had absolutely overcome everyone. As we stood there I was caught up in the spirit and told them what I was seeing. The Lord showed me a little child sitting in His lap and they sat together on a throne. He had His arms wrapped around the child in a sweet, protective, loving embrace.

In like fashion I wrapped my arms around the couple and then whispered to them, "Have you lost a child?" When they said "yes," they and the entire church began to release a great, broken sob. In that moment I realized this couple desperately needed a healing balm applied to their broken souls and wounded spirits. Had I not been sensitive to the Holy Spirit, or had any of the prophetic elements been out of order, it could have added unbelievable pain, hurt and sorrow to a family who was already dealing with more than they could bear.

Release the ministry with love and power.

Many other things were ministered to this couple in that meeting, and all of these words brought a much-needed release and healing to them and their church. The point being made is that seasoned prophets really understand God's timing and sensitivity on how to release what God shows them. These are the elements of true prophetic ministry, and they effectively release that ministry with the power, love and heart God intends.

How Prophets Function

Because prophets function like a pipeline between God and man, they become a conduit through which God speaks directly to people with clarity, power and authority. Another analogy is that prophets are designed to read the spiritual blueprint of someone's life. God shows what He intends to build them into and the prophet simply speaks what they read off that blueprint.

Prophets also speak to the seasons in the lives of people, cities, countries and nations. In connection with this they reveal the hidden truths and secrets of God for what He is doing during those times. Amos 3:7 speaks to this when it says;

> *"The Lord God does nothing unless he reveals His*
> *secret counsel to His servants the prophets."*

When you examine Scripture you can see how time and time again prophets were used by God to give clarity and vision about what was happening or would be happening in a given time period. Agabus in Acts spoke of a coming famine; Isaiah spoke of a coming captivity and national upheaval. Daniel spoke of global change and had insight about the end times we are living in, as did John. Joseph had prophetic revelation and insight on how to save Egypt. Other prophets spoke of revivals and the destinies of leaders or nations. Each time or season ordained by God had a corresponding prophet that spoke for what God was doing.

I had an interesting experience with this not long ago when I prophesied of a coming revival to Albany, NY. It happened during a meeting I was doing at Victory Church on Quail Street in downtown Albany. I spoke to the leaders of the church about an outpouring that God wanted to bring to that city and it would come in about a year. The pastor was to prepare them for what was to come.

Almost one year from when I gave that prophetic word a revival broke out on Quail Street and it lasted eight weeks. However during that revival I spoke a clear prophetic warning to the city. The Spirit of God said that if the other pastors of the city did not get behind what He was doing, He would lift and it would be over. Sad to say they did not listen and pastoral jealousy set in. Church walls went up so much that very few of the other pastors would come even though their people, and people from all over the country, did come. After eight weeks, things basically came to an abrupt end, and it was over.

God is the great communicator and He always desires to speak to His church. Because of this, prophets are always on call to reveal the mind of God to those they are sent to. They do not step in and out of their calling like they would take a shirt on and off. No matter where they are, they are still in that office. As such they are always able to read the spiritual blueprint of the people, church, region or nation they have been called to. How they do this will depend on the measure of authority they have and the way God communicates information specifically to and through them.

The prophet also functions as an ear to hear what God is saying, an eye to see what God is doing, a heart to feel what He is feeling and a mouth to say what He is speaking. Even with this, prophets do not know everything about every person, situation or season. They only know what God shows them, and can only speak what He releases them to say. This is why 1 Cor. 13:9 says; *"For we know in part, and we prophesy in part...."* The part God tells us to release will be released. The rest stays with the prophet or remains hidden in the heart of the Almighty.

Many times I have been given an insight or a revelation about something or someone, but the Lord told me to say nothing. In instances like this I have learned that it was either not the right time, not the right place or it was something God gave me to pray about. Just because you know something by the Spirit, does not mean you are to automatically speak it out. This is something very important every prophet must learn.

Proverbs 3:32 says, *"for the devious are an abomination to the Lord; but he is intimate with the upright."*(NASB) The word "intimate" in this passage is the Greek word "sod" which means a secret counsel, fellowship, friendship, an inner circle. Did you get that? Sometimes God reveals a secret to His prophets because He just wants to. He shares such things with those He trusts and considers to be in His inner circle. That's what friends do. They trust each other and share the intimate things of life together. What gets shared in these times is often not to be shared with others, and we must know the difference.

Prophets often speak about the ordained potential or destiny that God has planned for someone. However, genuine prophecy is never to be considered an absolute certainty. It is better described as the "divine possibilities" that are present within someone's life. This is because prophecy is a partnership between God, the prophet and the person who gets the word. The fulfillment of any word is dependent upon how well that person receives it, and how faithfully they cooperate with God from that point forward to obtain it.

As a person submits under authority and cooperates with the Holy Spirit, God Himself works to bring them to emotional, mental and spiritual maturity. If they allow these processes to develop their character, it will bring about personal growth, and spiritually position them to obtain His promise. Personal alignment and maturity is what allows every prophetic word to find its own expression in someone's life. Prophecy will unfold and fulfill itself as the one who got it continues to love and serve the Lord. However, if the process does not happen, no amount of personal effort or additional prophecy will bring God's design to pass in someone's life.

Change is required for a word to be fulfilled in your life.

As a prophet, I cannot stress strongly enough just how important this concept is. I have watched as magnificent words were spoken over people's lives and in that moment they were fired up to serve the Lord. Then, as time went on, and God required them to change, grow and develop, their passion evaporated. This in turn delayed the fulfillment of the word even more and eventually caused them to doubt it. Once doubt sets in it's basically all over, because doubt is the poison that kills any prophetic word.

I don't care what the calling is, or how powerful the gifts may be in your life, if you will not allow God to refine your character it will be to your eventual downfall. Worse than that, it will impact all those you were destined to touch. I saw this very thing bring one growing revival to a screeching halt not long ago. Just as it was getting started it abruptly ended, and only six of us knew exactly why.

There was an altercation that happened one afternoon between the worship leader who was called in to do the meetings, and the local pastor of a rapidly growing church. Things had really ignited, the meetings were packed out and there was an atmosphere of expectancy. After just five days there was a fire in the air that you could actually feel. Word was getting out and people were driving in from surrounding states to get into those meetings. Then one day a simple request was made by the pastor to safeguard his people from exhaustion, and that's when things fell apart.

The worship leader said he "knew how to run a revival" and he flat-out refused to listen to this godly pastor's concerns. He flew off in a rage and attacked the pastor's integrity in a most unexpected and dishonoring way. After that display of fleshy temper, the pastor dismissed the man on the spot, and they parted company. Without explanation to the crowds who were gathering, the revival was over just as it was about to explode. Because of this unrefined carnal nature, pride and the refusal to submit to authority, the entire region missed out on a greatly needed, fresh move of God.

Human nature kills great moves of God.

Many years ago I discovered that the devil knows the great killer of great words is human nature. Mix that with unrefined character and add in some delay, and you have a toxic cocktail that can kill anything. The reason is quite simple. When the average Saint gets a great prophetic word it requires great change to obtain it. However, our nature as humans is to be impatient and resist change. This in turn produces an automatic delay of the prophetic word. This delay allows the devil to tap into human thinking because he knows people tend to be impatient about everything. He then brings about discouragement, knowing that any form of discouragement always gives birth to doubt.

Remember, the things of God find their full expression in an atmosphere of faith and endurance. All the devil has to do is activate our natural tendencies and let things run their course. Our human capacity to refuse correction and resist change is well documented in church history. We want things now and don't want to submit to authority to get them. Thus, within us tends to be a deadly mix of immaturity, unteachableness and self-importance. These, and many other things, only serve to neutralize the genuine prophetic words that have been spoken over us. From this vantage point the devil has little to do but sit back, smile and watch us self-destruct. If someone fails to understand their own responsibility in unfolding a prophetic word, they will kill it before it ever has the chance to come to pass.

How ironic that the seed of it's own destruction is built right into the container that holds the prophetic word. This deadly reality is an ever-present danger and will negate the potential of any word you ever get. To ignore this fact is to sign the death certificate of every genuine prophecy you have received. Scripture makes it very clear that refusal to mature or cooperate with the Holy Spirit means the word will not manifest. The truth is that our life-long job is to see to it that our flesh does not direct the outcome of our spiritual life.

The Prophet's Reward

Matthew 10:41 says;

> *"He who receives a prophet in the name of a*
> *prophet shall receive a prophet's reward;..."*

The obvious question that must be asked related to the above scripture is, "What is a prophet's reward"? I have heard several good teachings in connection with this, but my own personal study and experience has given me a slightly different understanding of this verse. In essence, most people agree that a prophet's reward is the prophetic word they bring, and in part this is true. However the full reward a prophet brings is not just the prophetic word alone. There is more to the treasure within a prophet than just the word that gets released through them.

The fact is, a prophet's reward is the sum total of the kind of ministry they have, the character development they demonstrate and the level of intimacy and depth of relationship they have with the Lord. All these things have a profound impact as they are received by any church, and leave a deposit in the people of that place. This is the main reason why you must really know those who are speaking into your life or ministry.

The reward a prophet deposits into you as they minister depends more on who they are, and the condition of their heart, than it does on the accuracy of what they are saying. As a result, the reward that is left behind can either be good or bad, and few people understand this important principle. 1 Thes. 5:12 explains it this way:

> *"And we beseech you, brethren, to know them which labor*
> *among you, and are over you in the Lord, and admonish you;"*

The English word "know" in the above Scripture means "to be aware of or to consider, to know the lifestyle of, to perceive, understand and consider fully." When it comes to prophetic ministry, why is this so important? The answer is quite simple, if you think about it. There is a spiritual principle established in Scripture that states, "everything reproduces after its own kind, according to its own likeness." This can be found in Genesis 1:12 where we read;

"And the earth brought forth vegetation, plants yielding seed
after their kind, and trees bearing fruit, with seed in them, after
their kind; and God saw that it was good." Mat 7:20-23 adds
"So then, you will know them by their fruits. {21} "Not everyone
who says to Me, 'Lord, Lord,' will enter the kingdom of heaven;
but he who does the will of My Father who is in heaven."

Therefore, if a prophet is given the liberty to speak into your life and their own life is out of order, they will impart and reproduce that mess along with the word they give to you. The image a prophet broadcasts of themselves may not be who they really are. Impartation comes from the source of life not the image of it. A prophet who looks good on the outside but is messed up on the inside will mess up the one who receives an impartation from them. There is no other option since we always impart what is in us.

For the most part people never take note of or care about anything other than the operation of the gifting in a prophet's life. They will overlook and even excuse away character issues, wrong behavior, immaturity, rudeness, emotional instability and even open sin if a prophet can release clear, precise, accurate words. The outcome of this practice has been the demise of many ministries, and caused great disillusion among the Saints. God is not pleased with this practice and I am so glad that He is now exposing the rebellion and hidden sin in all who are called to five-fold ministry.

Bad character has been a destructive force in the Body of Christ since the church began. Take a brief look at the Corinthian church to confirm what I have just said. No church had more gifts evident and no church had more issues of sin evident as well. It is so important that we do not think one's ability to operate in the gifts confirms that they have a pure heart or good character. Nothing could be farther from the truth.

Active gifts are not evidence of a pure heart or good character.

In addition, the public disgrace that has come to many ministries has been the outcome of gift idol worship. God has exposed the sins of some of the most gifted ministers and it has rocked the church world. Adultery, drugs, homosexuality, embezzlement and a host of other fleshly manifestations have come to light. This has simply identified the real condition of the heart and purged the ministry to the core. God's purpose in all this has been to make His Church get their eyes off the gifts and ministers, and put their devotion back on Him.

I personally experienced an example of this very thing not long ago. I was ministering for the first time in a church in upstate of New York. The pastor was well loved, and as a second-generation minister he was carrying on his father's legacy. During the meeting I made what seemed to be a strange sidetrack and began to speak about an embezzlement situation that happened a few years back. Then during prophetic ministry at the end of the service I laid my hands on the pastor and began to prophesy about a great distress that was to come on him, his family and the church. When I finished my heart was broken and I noticed that his face had become a sickly, white color. The church wondered what in the world I was talking about, and the meeting ended on a cordial but very difficult note.

Within a few days I was called by several of the church members. Great fear had hit the church when that prophetic word had come to pass. The pastor had been fired from his job at a local bank and was arrested for the very thing I had spoken about. A television station even called me about the incident a day or so later. They wanted to interview me because my name had gotten out as the one who had spoken that prophetic word before it happened. I refused to comment and determined to love this brother and pray for his recovery. I knew God would never approve of me adding anything to the hurt and shame he, his family and his church were already feeling.

As I pondered this event, God reminded me of a word I had been given a number of years back by a respected minister. He said that God would bring me to the place as a prophet where He would trust me to go into the homes and churches of local, national and international leaders. My commission would be to bring private words of correction from the Lord to those who were in sin. Those who would listen and repent, God would heal and restore but those who would not, He would require me to publically expose. It would seem as if this has actually begun to happen.

As painful as it is, I thank God that this kind of thing is now happening on a regular basis in the Church. The exposure of sin has been changing the nature of ministry and the nature of ministers as well. It has become more like that which Jesus wants, and less like that which the world exalts. My prayer is that this purging continues until we all walk in humility and purity.

God has made it clear that character and rich personal relationship with Him, rather than gifting and speaking ability, are the things that validate authentic prophetic ministry. Our passion should be the same, and our heart cry should be for that kind of genuine innocence. As this happens, God will trust us with a heavier anointing, and in the end more powerful manifestations of His Kingdom will come to pass. In the final analysis this is how Jesus moved about, and it needs to be the way we move as well.

· · · · · · · · · · ·

**How Jesus
moved about
is the way we
should move
as well.**

· · · · · · · · · · ·

ACCURACY VERSES THE HEART OF GOD

atthew 7:22-23 makes a powerful point regarding the importance of having God's heart released when prophetic words are being spoken. All too often people have been enamored by the accuracy and clarity of a word but failed to see that it did not impart God's life to the one who received it. The Scripture below explains how this can happen.

> *"Many will say to Me on that day, 'Lord, Lord, did we not prophesy in Your name, and in Your name cast out demons, and in Your name perform many miracles?' "And then I will declare to them, 'I never knew you; depart from Me you who practice lawlessness.'"*

In this passage we see those who were involved with prophecy, deliverance and miracles. In fact the word "prophesy" here relates to the office of the prophet. These are all high level giftings that were quite impressive. These people were doing the works of God in a big way but they did not have the heart of God in what they did. Thus, they were not producing anything for God in what looked like very spiritual activity. I don't know about you, but this was very troubling to me when I first read it. However, after some study I began to see a profound truth that every prophet needs to understand.

First of all it is apparent that these people knew how to use their gifts and enter into what was clearly some type of ministry. There was prophecy, deliverance and miracles flowing in every direction. Apparently that was very impressive to man, but it seemed to hold no weight with God. He says that even though they did these things they never knew Him, and He did not know them.

The Greek word used for "knew" is "gnosis" which means "a first-hand intimate knowledge of." This means the gifts can actually operate at a very high level, even when people don't really know the giver of the gift. It is this lack of personal, heart knowledge that causes the Lord to reject the gifts and the ministry people think they have. This one revelation certainly put a new twist on the importance of relational intimacy with God for me. I realized that without it He does not recognize any minister or ministry as valid.

What we see here in shocking detail is that someone can learn to use the gifts of God without being in deep personal relationship with Him. Where there is no genuine connection to Jesus, and no prayer life that accompanies the operation of the gifts, God is not glorified. Thus people can actually learn to powerfully operate in any gift but it can be devoid of His nature, lacking His heart and empty of any spiritual life. As disturbing as this may seem, it does happen and we must be aware of it. God never recognizes such ministry and He does not acknowledge those who operate in the Kingdom this way.

Using His gifts without being in relationship with Him is spiritual prostitution.

What the Lord spoke to me many years ago is that using the gifts without being in relationship with Him is nothing more than spiritual prostitution. How sad it is when people want the benefit and recognition of ministry without having the deep commitment and personal connection necessary to keep it pure. God never honors those who do such things and prophetic ministry that is built on gifting alone will not produce anything of lasting value. It will not meet with God's approval and those who function this way are ultimately going to be identified as those who "practice lawlessness."

Matthew 12:36 gives us additional insight into the heart of God in this important matter when it says;

> *"But I say unto you, that every idle word (Gk."argos*
> *rhema") that men shall speak, they shall give*
> *account thereof in the day of judgment.*

The *"argos rhema"* that is mentioned here is a specific Greek term. It means that something can be technically accurate but impotent, powerless and lacking the life of God. Thus a prophecy that started as a "rhema" word from God can end up powerless, empty, void of His Spirit and lacking His life. Such words accomplish nothing and those who give them will not be accepted before the Lord.

What becomes clear is that true prophecy is not based upon how accurate a word is. It is more about releasing something from the heart of God through a well-developed character. It is something that touches and imparts His life into the very core of someone's being. True prophecy has always been about delivering what God says, when He says it, with His heart. The bottom line is simple. Genuine prophecy flows best from faithful ambassadors who keep their personality, ideas, emotions and thoughts separate from what the Lord says, so that they correctly represent the One who sent them.

When God's Ambassadors Misrepresent Him

In Exodus 17:6 we read:

> *"Behold, I will stand before you there on the rock at Horeb; and you shall strike the rock, and water will come out of it, that the people may drink." And Moses did so in the sight of the elders of Israel."*

Because he obeyed God, Moses and the people were all blessed at this point in their journey. Water came out and their thirst was satisfied. However, the next time Israel wanted water, a huge mistake was made. This is a classic example from Scripture of God's ambassador misrepresenting Him. It is found in Numbers 20:1-12(NASB). An in-depth look at this key passage will help you see the importance of this critical issue. Here we read;

> *"Then the sons of Israel, the whole congregation, came to the wilderness of Zin in the first month; and the people stayed at Kadesh. Now Miriam died there and was buried there. And there was no water for the congregation; and they assembled themselves against Moses and Aaron. The people thus contended with Moses and spoke, saying, "If only we had perished when our brothers perished before the LORD! "Why then have you brought the LORD'S assembly into this wilderness, for us and our beasts to die here? "And why have you made us come up from Egypt, to bring us in to this wretched place? It is not a place of grain or figs or vines or pomegranates, nor is there water to drink." Then Moses and Aaron came in from the presence of the assembly to the doorway of the tent of meeting, and fell on their faces. Then the glory of the LORD appeared to them; and the LORD spoke to Moses, saying, "Take the rod; and you and your brother*

Aaron assemble the congregation and speak to the rock before their
eyes, that it may yield its water. You shall thus bring forth water
for them out of the rock and let the congregation and their beasts
drink." So Moses took the rod from before the LORD, just as He had
commanded him; and Moses and Aaron gathered the assembly before
the rock. And he said to them, "Listen now, you rebels; shall we
bring forth water for you out of this rock?" Then Moses lifted up his
hand and struck the rock twice with his rod; and water came forth
abundantly, and the congregation and their beasts drank. But the
LORD said to Moses and Aaron, "Because you have not believed Me,
to treat Me as holy in the sight of the sons of Israel, therefore you shall
not bring this assembly into the land which I have given them.""

In the above passage we see Moses once again performing a mighty miracle. For a second time he is told by God to bring forth water out of the rock so that the children of Israel can satisfy their thirst and their animals can drink. However, God tells Moses to speak to the rock this time. Instead, Moses strikes the rock, but true to His own nature, God still supplies for His people and water comes pouring out. Everybody is satisfied and Moses is a hero in the eyes of the people, but he is not so heroic in the eyes of God. In fact, God says his actions have prematurely ended his life and he will no longer be the one who will take God's people into the Promised Land.

What in the world did Moses do that made God so upset with him? Knowing the answer to that question may very well be the most important thing you will learn from this chapter. Pay close attention to what follows. What you discover could be the thing that prevents you from destroying your own ministry and credibility with God.

For one thing Moses did not do what God said. This time Moses was told to *"speak to the rock,"* not strike it. This is a very important detail.

In striking the rock a second time Moses broke the Old Testament type or shadow that was designed to point to Christ. The Bible says in 1 Cor. 10:4 that Jesus was the rock that followed them in the wilderness. He was the rock they all drank from and were satisfied. Scripture is very clear in that Jesus, our rock, was only to be struck or killed once. In fact 1 Peter 3:18 says Jesus died once for all mankind.

When Moses struck the rock this second time, he broke the Old Testament "type." God intended this to be something that would point directly to what Jesus did for us. Our Rock was only struck once for our salvation. We simply need to come to Him and repent. In that repentance all we have to do is speak to the Rock and ask for forgiveness. We can then drink the water of salvation that flows from Him. But, by striking the rock this second time, Moses made a huge blunder that stirred the anger of God and it cost him dearly.

Secondly Moses was the one who was fed up and angry with the people, while God was not. The anger of Moses spilled out when he called them rebels. From this place of frustration he misrepresented the heart of God. As an ambassador he was never to go to the people with anything but God's heart, and God's attitude. The moment his own emotions got in the way, he caused the people to believe something about God that was not true. This was a major breach of trust between him and the Lord. This misrepresentation was a second thing that cost him his future ministry and inheritance.

Every prophet is called to be an ambassador for God. They are given the responsibility of speaking for God and into the lives of His people. If they discharge that responsibility with a heart, character or mind that is connected to Him, all is well. However, if their relationship with God is shallow and undeveloped, and their thoughts and emotions do not reflect God's, this poses a massive problem. The ministry of an immature or undeveloped prophet, will not only bring destruction to them, it will also mislead God's people and cause them to think He is something He's not.

This is the reason God spends so much time working on the character, heart and mind of those called as prophets. Look at the life of Joseph, Jacob, Moses and David, to name just a few. Each was a prophet with a huge call on their life, but each also had massive issues that needed to be refined. God used many difficult life experiences to change them, shape them, build them up and make them equal to the call He placed on them.

Thirdly, by striking the rock rather than speaking to it, Moses broke a second type as well. Speaking to the rock was to represent a second New Testament experience. The baptism in the Holy Spirit is all about speaking. That is, after salvation we can come to the rock, Jesus, and receive the baptism in the Holy Spirit. That baptism releases a river of living water that flows out of our inner most being and we speak in tongues. When Moses failed to speak to the rock he broke this second Old Testament type.

By his words and actions, Moses ended up disobeying God, misrepresenting God's heart and he destroyed two powerful Old Testament "types." Because of this he lost a great deal of what God intended to give him. In addition, he brought his own ministry to a premature and rapid end. It becomes painfully clear that misrepresenting God is one of the key elements of false prophecy. It is as much a matter of the heart, the attitude and the way that something is delivered, as it is the actual words that are being spoken.

Misrepresenting God brought Moses' ministry to a premature end.

Until a prophet grasps the significance of knowing God's heart in what is said, they will never be able to really know and release God's will to His people. If you are serious about your ministry as a prophet you had better be serious about these important issues. Until you can connect

God's words to His heart, then releasing His will with purity, clarity and power will never happen.

Having a tender heart when delivering a word is so important. I realized this one day when I was ministering in Albany, NY. During that meeting I was about to wrap up the time of ministry and at the last moment my eye was drawn to the last row of the church. There sat a man and next to him the row was filled with people from the age of young adults to young children. I called the man forward and then realized all the other people were his family, so they all came forward at the same time.

As they reached about the halfway point to the front, a sense of great loss and sorrow began to overwhelm me and I began to prophesy to that end. He and his family began to cry as I spoke the word of the Lord over them and it blessed all of them. After this the meeting ended and my wife and I headed for home. During the week I was in prayer and this man came to mind. At some point I was snatched up in the Spirit and found myself standing on what looked like liquid pearls. About 30 feet from me was the Lord with His arm wrapped around the shoulder of a young woman. She was slender, had long straight hair, big eyes and a wonderful laugh like that of a teenager.

She was looking at Jesus and then they both looked at me. In that moment I could hear her voice say within me, "What are you doing here?" to which I responded, "I don't even know where here is." She looked at Jesus again and at that moment I began leaving this place. She then turned to me and said "Tell him…" and then she blew me a kiss good-by. The next week I was back in the same church and when I saw the man I explained to him what I had experienced. He and all those with him began to laugh and cry almost uncontrollably.

What I didn't know was that I had described his wife the way she looked in their wedding picture. She had just died of cancer and it happened one morning while she was home from the hospital. The man had stepped out for a moment to make them breakfast and it was then that she died. He and his wife always said good-bye to one another throughout all the years they had been married. He had been grieving that loss because she had slipped away so quickly and they never got to say good-bye. Yet in His love and mercy, God allowed it to happen even after death had come. Because my heart was tender before God, He trusted me to deliver this life-giving last message to those who so desperately needed it.

In the final analysis, every prophet is called to be God's representative to His people. As Bill Johnson says, a representative is called to "re-present" God to those who don't know Him or His ways. My prayer for you in closing this chapter is that you will grow to the place where His heart is found in all you do, and this brings His ministry through you with great love and adoration to a broken and hurting world. There is no higher calling and no better place for any prophet to live.

. . . .

**May God's
heart be found
in all you do.**

. . . .

PROPHETIC OPERATION

Prophecy is not a "one size fits all" kind of thing. God is a God of variety and He gives to each according to His own design. As a result, the Word of God makes it clear that prophecy has many different levels of operation and many different applications in the Body of Christ. I have seen those who did not understand these basic truths spend a great deal of time and effort trying to be something, or do something God never intended.

In the material that follows I have done my best to provide an overview of the different kinds of prophetic operation. Please realize that this is not the last word on the subject, but it may shed some light in areas where you need additional clarity. Since prophecy is ministered in many different ways and in a number of different settings, this overview will establish a clear framework from which to view how prophecy can be released in the Church.

The Prophetic Presbytery Meeting

Prophetic presbytery, as we know it today, was reintroduced to the Church in 1948 during a revival that broke out in Canada. A minister by the name of Reg Lazell was one of the fathers of that prophetic movement when it was first restored. In those early days genuine prophets were very rare. In addition, prophetic presbytery teams were few and far between. They were so rare in fact that people only expected to receive that level of prophetic ministry once in their life. Today much has changed and in churches that embrace this ministry, people can expect to receive prophetic presbytery a number of times during their lifetime.

This ministry, when released by qualified prophets, has proven to be invaluable in building up people and especially in building up the local church. Prophetic presbytery requires a very special kind of prophetic teamwork if it is to have maximum impact on the local church. Because of this, not all prophets are suited for this specific ministry.

What we learn from Scripture is that some prophets may typically operate alone, while others are called to work in tandem. Those prophets who can work well with others will at times be called to form a team to minister prophetic presbytery with the laying on of hands. Such teams are clearly identified in 1 Timothy 4:14. Here we read;

> *"Neglect not the gift that is in thee, which was given thee by prophecy, with the laying on of the hands of the presbytery."*

The prophetic presbytery team mentioned above not only prophesied over young Timothy but they also imparted spiritual gifts to him, and Paul tells Timothy not to neglect those gifts. In addition, in 1Tim 1:18, Paul told Timothy he was to use the prophecies spoken over him to "fight a good fight." Using those prophesies, he was to do strong warfare against the devil whenever he attacked the young man's faith, destiny or place in ministry. He wrote;

> *"This command I entrust to you, Timothy, my son, in*
> *accordance with the prophecies previously made concerning*
> *you, that by them you may fight the good fight,"*

Thus, when a true prophecy is released to someone by a prophetic presbytery team, the devil will come and try to steal, kill and destroy that word from them. As was said earlier, doubt, delay and distraction are the biggest enemies of any prophetic word. Each person will have to fight for what God spoke over them to see it come to pass. It is the power of a clear, strong word spoken in prophetic presbytery that gives people the weapons they need to beat the enemy in this deadly warfare. This is one reason why prophetic presbytery is so important in the life of the Church, and in the spiritual life of the people who receive it.

The Prophetic Presbytery Team

Prophetic presbytery teams work in a very unique and specific way. Because of this, only the senior pastor of a local church has the authority to invite such a team in to do this specific kind of meeting. In essence the job of the team is to supernaturally confirm and identify the ministry, gifts and callings of specific individuals in the church. This serves to set them into the foundation of the local church and helps the leadership identify and establish other ministries as well. Most of all, it serves to bring a greater clarity and order to the congregation in general.

A prophetic presbytery team works spiritually in a highly ordered way to establish, build and release the members of a church into their destiny. This is one reason why it is so important for a local pastor to trust who is on that team and who in the church will receive their ministry. For this reason I usually suggest to pastors that they contact the lead prophet and let that person put the actual presbytery team together. That prophet will know who they flow best with. I have been invited to be on teams with prophets I never worked with before, and for the most part it went well. Needless to say the pastor has the right and authority to put together a team of prophets they know and trust. However, this is not always the best way to set up such a vitally important ministry.

Receiving Prophetic Presbytery

To begin with, those being prophesied over are pre-selected by the leadership before the meeting begins. Usually these people are in need of more direction, additional conformation or greater clarification regarding their area of ministry or life calling. In addition they must meet certain qualifications as established by the leadership of the church. Beyond this they must receive instruction about what to expect during those meetings. In this way they are fully prepared to receive the kind of detailed prophecy that will be spoken, and this helps them find their place in the local church.

The prophetic presbytery team itself will consist of two or perhaps three prophets. If the team has three, two will be prophets and the third is often an apostle who has well developed spiritual gifts. This is because Ephesians 2:20 says apostles and prophets are called to build the foundation of the church. The team itself must flow as one and the ministers must have ministry styles that complement and enhance each other. When a presbytery team flows like this it allows for the release of balanced, clear words over those who are receiving the ministry.

A prophetic presbytery team comes to read the spiritual blueprint of those who are committed to that specific local church. They come to clarify personal callings, confirm ministries, point out areas of strength and identify areas that need change. In this spiritual environment, a presbytery team can impart spiritual gifts by the laying on of hands, according to 2 Timothy 1:6 and 1 Timothy 4:14-15. In addition, they can identify and activate what is already present in people in order to confirm and release a much-needed ministry into that local church.

During these meetings the team may identify past events in a person's life that still hinders them in the present. Deep wounds, personal tragedy or places of brokenness can be used by the devil to keep people bound and robbed of their destiny. Mature prophets who are functioning well together will often address such issues and bring great healing and deliverance to those who need to be set free.

As for the presbytery meeting itself, the basic format is simple. A brief dynamic time of praise and worship will happen first which fires up the spiritual environment. After this, pre-selected people are called forward, either singles or couples, and they are invited to sit in chairs that face the congregation. This is called a "setting." The team of prophets then gathers around those seated and one at a time they begin to prophesy the word of the Lord over them.

The length of the prophecies being spoken over each "setting" usually lasts 20 to 30 minutes in total. As a result, the number of meetings needed depends on the ministry style of the prophets and the number of people who will receive prophetic ministry at each meeting. If the words run long, fewer people will receive ministry and more meetings will be required. If the words are shorter in length more people will be ministered to and fewer meetings will be needed.

My experience in doing prophetic presbytery over the years has shown that not more than seven or eight settings per meeting are best to be done. Since each person will receive twenty to thirty minutes of prophetic ministry this means that three or more hours of actual prophecy will be released in each meeting. Even for seasoned prophets this many hours of ministry can be a drain on their physical and emotional resources.

Because of this it is important for local pastors to honor the prophets and not wear the team out by pulling in extra people at the last minute.

Prophetic presbytery is designed to be a blessing for the whole church. Lengthy meetings can also impact the congregation adversely. People still have to work, get to bed and care for their families. If the presbytery meeting runs long it will tend to wear them out and fewer people will show up to participate. This is not a good thing since prophetic presbytery is designed to be a blessing for the whole church. Because of this the whole church should be present when people are being prophesied over.

Who Should Get This Ministry?

Those who are candidates to receive prophetic presbytery must be solid, faithful, tithing members of the local church. In this way the leadership can look for a directive or a confirming word about them in order to establish them and their place in that body. New people to the church, visitors and those who are uncommitted or unfaithful in their walk with God are never a candidate for this specific kind of ministry.

The purpose of prophetic presbytery is to set people into the body who can help carry the load. It is never used as a spiritual counseling session to make people emotionally whole, financially responsible or personally mature. Using presbytery for this is contrary to its intended purpose. In fact, giving this kind of ministry to people who are in need of such things will cause them and the church great trouble. I have seen pastors violate this principle time and time again only to be sorry down the road. For a more detailed look at this concept please get a copy of my book "Preparing For Prophetic Presbytery."

Beyond prophetic presbytery, there are several other types of prophetic ministry mentioned in Scripture. Like prophetic presbytery, each of these has their proper place and specific purpose in the church. It is important to fully understand how they work and what each is designed to do. I have seen great confusion come into a church because people don't know what the parameters are for each kind of meeting, or what level of prophetic ministry is appropriate in each setting. What follows is a brief overview of these other kinds of prophetic meetings.

The Open Meeting

The open meeting is what most people think of when they speak about having prophetic ministry. This style of ministry is the most common method seen in the church. The old time Pentecostal preachers used this almost exclusively, so most of the church is familiar with how this kind of meeting is conducted. Kenneth Hagin, Kathryn Kuhlman and Kim Clement are examples of ministers who have used the open meeting format and it has worked well for their style of ministry.

In this setting there is worship and the word of God is usually ministered first. Then the prophet selects people by "calling them out" of the congregation. This style of ministry is often a more general level of prophecy and is usually not highly directive in nature. At times it can be very specific, but that kind of specificity is best utilized when it is reserved for prophetic presbytery. The word of knowledge, word of wisdom and healing are more likely to be released in this kind of meeting.

As a general rule, identifying a new ministry or a life calling should not be released in this setting unless that person's spiritual oversight is present to hear and confirm what is being said. The reason for this is quite simple. No prophet has the authority or right to randomly place this prophetic "seed" into the sheep of another shepherd. They must have permission from the person's spiritual oversight to do so. That is God's Biblical order and prophets need to honor it.

When a higher level of prophecy is released without the agreement or the knowledge of the person's oversight, it is a gross violation of the spiritual life of the person, and it dishonors the pastor's God-given line of authority. If a prophet takes that kind of liberty, spiritual intimacy has occurred that has the potential to bring great confusion to the person and do damage to them and the relationship they have with their local church.

Why is that? Let's look at Judges 14:18 to put all this in a Biblical perspective. Here we read:

> *"… And he said to them, "If you had not plowed with my heifer, You would not have found out my riddle."*

The truth that Samson releases is very profound. These men went to Samson's wife without his permission or knowledge. They usurped his authority and connected to his wife in such a way that actually undermined his leadership and hindered what God was asking Him to do.

In the same way, those who put prophetic "seed" into another's sheep without the oversights agreement have usurped that spiritual authority. In addition they have violated the trust that sheep has with their shepherd.

Every prophet must honor the spiritual authority God has set in place.

This ends up giving birth to illegitimate ministry that will go unrecognized and may remain unvalued by the spiritual authority. The end result is that everyone is harmed because the prophet did not honor the spiritual authority or the spiritual lines that God had set in place.

This is why I believe people should never be prophesied into ministry or given specific directive words in an open meeting unless their pastor is present. We have seen massive confusion unleashed when well-intentioned prophets spoke directive words to individuals when their leadership was not there. Since no one in authority was there to verify, confirm or support what was said, it was never going to find its full expression.

This is such a big issue because people who get these words often attempt to move on them and start a ministry based upon what was said, without the knowledge or agreement of their leadership. Worse yet, they may do so with no clear understanding of the vision of their local church. Nothing could be more destructive to someone's walk in God, or detrimental to the trust that exists between the sheep and shepherd.

By acting this way, the person is actually trying to birth a ministry that should not and will not be recognized by the leadership of the church. This may even be in conflict with other ministries of the church that have the backing and support of the leadership. Such a ministry is called "illegitimate" because it was conceived outside the church family and without the knowledge, training or blessing of the leaders God set in place over them. Such ministry is a dishonor to the church leadership and a betrayal of their trust.

Never forget, the local leaders are those God called to work with, develop, train and release people so they can fulfill any prophetic word. Because of this, they must know what is being spoken and who is doing the speaking. They must identify how that word fits with the vision of the house and the calling on the person's life. If the leadership is not present when a directive word is given then someone has "plowed with another man's heifer" and this always produces illegitimate ministry. Such ministry will usually end up being unrecognized in the local church and this serves to bring confusion, hurt and rejection to everyone involved.

There are a few mature prophets we know and trust that do operate with great accuracy as individuals. They have spoken directive words to us in open meetings and for the most part have been right on target. However, all these ministers deeply respect, and willingly submit under the authority of the local church. They are not "lone rangers" looking to put a few more notches on their spiritual six-shooter. They are mature ministers who flow in clear, accurate levels of prophecy and each has a proven ministry that operates with the trust of local leadership.

A Second Type Of Open Meeting

Another possibility for an open meeting is when a prophet in attendance is given the opportunity to minister a word, even though it is not their meeting. Two such examples found in Scripture occurred with the prophet Agabus. In Acts 11:27-28 and Acts 21:10-11 we see this in operation. Here we read the following:

> *"Now at this time some prophets came down from Jerusalem to Antioch. And one of them named Agabus stood up and began to indicate by the Spirit that there would certainly be a great famine all over the world. And this took place in the reign of Claudius."*
> *"And as we were staying there for some days, a certain prophet named Agabus came down from Judea. And coming to us, he took Paul's belt and bound his own feet and hands, and said, "This is what the Holy Spirit says: 'In this way the Jews at Jerusalem will bind the man who owns this belt and deliver him into the hands of the Gentiles.'"*

In these instances Agabus was a well know, proven prophet. In both cases it was not his meeting, but he was given the opportunity to release God's heart to those who needed it. The Bible tells us his words proved to be correct and changed the course of life for many people. Thus a seasoned prophet will often step into these deeper realms and deliver God's Word, even when it might not be considered the "normal" order since it was not their meeting.

The kind of prophetic ministry found in open meetings is best designed to encourage, buildup and edify those whom God singles out of the crowd. The prophet will "scan" the people looking for those God is pointing out and then identifies them. The person may stay seated, stand up or be called out of their seat to come down front so they can be ministered to. However the prophet does it, it will be appropriate for the person and the setting of the meeting.

The open meeting has been a standard form of prophetic ministry for many years, and it is still a valid form of ministry today. As prophets of God move by the Spirit, they can release a great blessing to those God wants to touch. In its proper place, the open meeting will always play a vital role in ministering to the needs of the Body of Christ.

Prophets moving by the Spirit release great blessing to those God wants to touch.

Ordination

Ordination is another kind of prophetic meeting. At an ordination, the ordaining spiritual oversight, along with invited trusted prophets, will lay hands on those who are called and set apart for the work of the ministry. Specific, clear directive words are often released to further identify, clarify and confirm the call on that person. This is usually an official ceremony that marks the beginning of someone's full appointment and release into five-fold ministry.

We see clear examples of this in Acts 13:1-3 and Titus 1:5.

"Now there were at Antioch, in the church that was there,
prophets and teachers: Barnabas, and Simeon who was called
Niger, and Lucius of Cyrene, and Manaen who had been
brought up with Herod the tetrarch, and Saul. And while
they were ministering to the Lord and fasting, the Holy Spirit
said, "Set apart for Me Barnabas and Saul for the work to
which I have called them." Then, when they had fasted and
prayed and laid their hands on them, they sent them away."
"For this cause left I thee in Crete, that thou shouldest
set in order the things that are wanting, and ordain
elders in every city, as I had appointed thee:"

Should a ministry be ordained or licensed?

Most churches ordain their own ministers once they bear consistent fruit. However, the individual being considered for this is often "licensed" first. It should be noted that no such practice is ever found in the Bible but it has found great acceptance in the Church today. A ministry license officially recognizes the personal call on someone without releasing them on their own. Their church or an overseeing apostolic covering usually gives this. Local and state governing authorities will accept a ministry license when issued this way. This license allows someone to have access to otherwise restricted areas so they can function in their calling and prove their ministry while still being under the direct supervision of the local church.

In theory, a person should be licensed when they have developed their gifts and ministry, and proven themselves faithful to their calling. Those who develop a proven ministry will be ordained and released fully into that calling at a later time. This is part of the reason why Jesus said: *"many are called but few are chosen."* Those who answer the call will only be chosen once they have endured and proven themselves faithful. As ministry is developed and produces lasting fruit, ordination will quite naturally follow.

To officially ordain anyone without this important first step has resulted in a lot of confusion over the years. Until an individual has proven themselves faithful to their calling, and faithful to their oversight, they are not ready to be launched out on their own. Only time and trials prove a ministry. Even if there are great gifts evident, these are of secondary value. Proven character and true loyalty must be developed first in those who have also demonstrated genuine endurance. Once these qualities are evident, ordination is well deserved and will be highly valued.

Many religious organizations have placed additional requirements on those who want to be ordained. Some require a specific level of college education and additional time in an internship program as well. Once these are successfully completed the overseeing organization will ordain the candidate. For the most part, this kind of ordination is only good within the specific denomination that is connected to the college issuing the theological degree.

While education is a good thing, such ordinations may not be based upon an actual calling, and this poses a number of problems. The biblical standard for ordination is consistent, lasting fruit, not educational background. I believe this practice has contributed a great deal to the lack of power that is present in many denominations today. Men have elected to "go into the ministry" as an occupation and not a calling from God. As a result we now have professional ministers who oversee congregations that are basically social clubs. These ministers lack the power, purity, endurance and personal conviction needed to develop a vibrant church of mature, strong believers.

Please understand that I am in favor of education and have taken many classes taught by anointed bible teachers. CLEN (Christian Life

Educator's Network) is a Bible college network designed to bring anointed teaching directly into the church or home of those who want to further their education. This was founded by Dr. Ron Cottle a number of years ago and has been very beneficial in developing my spiritual life. Our church actually had a CLEN/CLST campus for a number of years and we hope to have one again. That being said, college classes do not qualify anyone to be licensed or ordained. Only fruit produced in a specific area of calling opens the door for legitimate release into five-fold ministry.

Chamber Prophecy

Chamber prophecy is another form of prophetic ministry found in the Bible. In chamber prophecy there is a one-on-one meeting between a seasoned prophet and the person who receives the word. This style of ministry has its roots in 2 Kings 20. Here the prophet Isaiah goes into King Hezekiah's bedchamber. Hezekiah is mortally ill and he is expected to die. However, the prophet privately delivers the word of the Lord to him and when he received it, he repented and his life was extended for fifteen years.

Today there are two styles of chamber prophecy being done, and these are usually found at conferences. The first is where people sign a list and are invited into a room with a seasoned prophet who gives them the word of the Lord. In these settings the prophet may have an apprentice with them. This person is under the prophet's authority and stands there for the purpose of prophetic training. The seasoned prophet leads out and then offers the apprentice an opportunity to share what they have received from the Lord.

The pastor of those receiving such words is usually not present in this setting. Because of this, the word given should be, clear, edifying and non-directive in nature. It will most often be a word of encouragement, edification, confirmation and comfort to the ones who come. Often the gift of prophecy, word of knowledge and word of wisdom are what is flowing in these settings. No one should ever be prophesied into a ministry or have their life redirected through this kind of ministry.

When I have done this style of prophetic ministry and God gave me a more directive type of word, I always called for the individual's pastor to come into the room. I explain privately to the pastor what God had shown me and then asked permission to give that word to their congregation member. If permission was granted I released the word. If the pastor felt the person was not ready for the word, I would tell the pastor but not the individual. By doing things in this order, the pastor could work with the individual involved and make sure that legitimate ministry was birthed at the right time.

The second kind of chamber prophecy, called "conference prophecy," is a bit different from the above. In this case people are assigned or sign up to receive ministry that is made available to them during some time slot at a conference. This is inaccurately called "prophetic" ministry since it usually will not involve those who are in the office of the prophet. In this setting people are sent to small rooms, cubicles or corners of a room where basic supervision is provided and a minimal level of training has been given to those doing the actual speaking.

Those learning how to operate in various gifts of the Spirit are allowed to practice giving words to those who sign up. What is said is in the order of edification, exhortation and comfort with some words of knowledge or words of wisdom mixed in. Individual pastoral oversight is never present, so those who may be in authority over the people receiving the words have no input or idea as to what is being spoken over the members of their congregation. Unfortunately this is the most common but definitely not the most accurate or biblically sound form of ministry.

I have been involved in such settings over the years and seen the benefit and the many issues that arise. I was on teams for two years with Morning

Star Ministries at conferences in Charlotte, NC. I also did the training and set up the teams for the annual Maranatha Ministerial Fellowship International Fall conference in Williston, Vermont for quite a few years. Of the two, I felt most confident and secure with the ministry that was done under MMFI. This is because I personally met with, mentored and trained all the people who were going to be on the ministry teams.

I spent personal time with those who qualified, and then handpicked the teams based upon the gift-mix and callings that were evident in each individual. In this environment I was able to provide a much higher measure of spiritual safety, training and purity of delivery with those doing the speaking. In addition there was a much greater measure of security for those who signed up to receive what was said.

This second type of chamber prophecy should be received with the greatest level of caution. For the most part, there is no control over who is allowed to speak, and no guarantee about the spiritual purity of what is said. Those who sit under such ministry must be aware of this, and be on guard.

Caution should be exercised when receiving conference prophecy.

Consider this, you could be receiving an impartation from someone who has a prophetic gift but is in rebellion to authority, emotionally unstable, sexually impure and has caused a split in their local church. Yet, because of the gift they have, they are allowed on a team and will be sanctioned to put that foul spiritual mixture into all who have signed up. What kind of a mess do you think they might impart into the lives of unsuspecting people who receive that ministry?

In these situations the biggest safeguard you have is to record every word, write them out on paper, and then carefully review them with your local leadership. To not do so puts you in a very dangerous place indeed. Untested, unknown people speaking from an unknown source have the potential to impart a huge mess into your life. Unless there is verification and clarification of every aspect of these words, they should be considered invalid and basically thrown out.

Naturally, you should never consider words of this type to be on equal ground or at the same level of authority as those given by seasoned prophets, or those spoken over you in prophetic presbytery. Conference prophecy does not have the same spiritual authority and should not be used to do spiritual warfare in the same way as a valid word from seasoned prophets.

Conference prophecy can however, be beneficial to bring confirmation and edification to new believers. This kind of ministry is best used to encourage those who have not yet learned to hear the voice of God. In addition, this ministry encourages those doing the speaking because it demonstrates they can learn to hear God's voice and are able to speak it out as a blessing to those who need it.

. . . .

**Prophetic
words are not
all equal.**

. . . .

Establishing New Prophets

A s I was coming up through the ranks, I had no one to mentor me at my very beginning stages. My pastor was a wonderful man but he was just learning about his own apostolic ministry, and was trying to develop that call in his life. He often did not understand me as a young prophet, and did not know what to do to harness and develop my calling. Because of this I spent many years frustrating him and floundering in mistakes that destroyed my own credibility.

God eventually orchestrated my life so that I was personally connected to seasoned prophets who could do for me what others could not. Through this process I came to see the great advantage gained by those who did receive prophetic mentoring on a personal level. This is one reason why God led my wife and I to establish the PDM network. This network is built upon the Ephesians 2:20 model and through it we hope to develop a clear way to identify, encourage, build up, guide and release those called to prophetic ministry. For more information on our network please go to our website, www.pdministry.org and click on the "PDM Network" link.

Before our network was set up I made it a part of our ministry to assist young prophets when we could. Those who are called to the prophetic arena and have a clear, strong flow, often have no opportunity to use what they have. Their potential ministry and gifts remain undeveloped to their frustration, and what they do have is often used incorrectly to the detriment of their ministry.

Young prophets need training.

God gave me a simple solution to this problem. I used it during those times I was ministering in prophetic presbytery, or doing open meetings. He instructed me to use those events to develop young prophets and help them find their prophetic flow. In fact we still use this strategy today on occasion with those who may not be part of our network but still need the opportunity to develop their calling.

When I was asked to put together a presbytery team or to go to another church to do prophetic ministry, I invited a young prophet, an "Elisha," to meet me there for the purpose of providing instruction and training. The "Elisha" sat alongside me and got under the anointing that was present. They were never actually a part of the ministry team, but they were given the opportunity, and proper guidance, to release what God was showing them when it was appropriate. In this way they came under my prophetic mantle and it safely stirred up the ministry they had.

I found this to be a very effective way to develop those who have a call to prophetic ministry but don't have the opportunity to exercise it, or be trained in their local church. This experience has proven quite valuable to those who accepted the invitation and I encourage other prophets to find an "Elisha" to build into. Not only does it establish others in their calling, but more importantly, it builds up the Body of Christ. This experience is beneficial to all involved and I highly recommend it.

Some Simple Guidelines For An "Elisha"

Having worked with the "Elisha" concept for a number of years, I suggest the following guidelines to help make the experience productive and enjoyable for everyone involved.

1. Identify an "Elisha" by asking pastors of the churches you are associated with who they believe has a calling as a prophet.

2. Ask the pastor if they will release this individual occasionally to receive training. You must ask because you do not have the authority to feed and lead the sheep of another shepherd.

3. Notify any church you are going to that you are inviting this person to join you. A pastor may have a concern about it and they need the opportunity to express this before you arrive to do ministry. Make it clear that the "Elisha" will not be an expense to the church. They are simply joining you at the location but it is their responsibility to arrive on time and provide their own food and/or lodging as needed.

4. Before the meeting, explain exactly how and when you want them to function. They do not have the authority or right to just jump in and speak whenever they want. Clear guidelines ahead of time will prevent them from being uncertain about what to do and it will prevent them from making mistakes. Most of all it will stop them from causing confusion during any ministry time. Explain that they have been invited to be under your mantle for training purposes only. This is not an endorsement of their ministry because only their oversight has the authority and personal relationship with them to provide that.

5. Make it clear to them and the pastor of the church that they are not part of the ministry team and will not receive any part of the

offering. Offerings always go to the prophet that is called in to do the meeting.

6. After every meeting, set aside a specific time to evaluate and instruct the "Elisha." This must be direct and honest communication. It will provide encouragement, guidance, instruction and correction as needed. If they spoke in any meeting, the evaluation must address specific points such as ineffective personal ministry styles, inaccuracies, unclear deliveries, things that worked well, personal strengths and weaknesses. If a young prophet cannot embrace and fully accept this kind of instruction they are not ready to be trained.

7. When the ministry time is concluded, get with the pastor of the "Elisha" to go over everything they did. Encourage the pastor to find ways to help the person develop their gifts and ministry. Help the pastor understand when and how the gifts should operate in their church. Especially clarify at what level the individual is operating. This will be particularly helpful for them in finding their place of full expression within their local church.

If all goes well, you may ask that same individual to join you again in the future. By doing so, you can build a relationship with them and their pastor. Through this kind of relational **Relational connections open ministry potential.** connection you open ministry potential and may end up being a spiritual father to them or even to their church. This is the highest calling of every five-fold minister. By being a father in the faith to those who trust us, we grow the church and release people into their destiny in God's Kingdom.

Taking the time to develop the next generation of prophetic ministry is of vital importance to the church. The fact is, unless there is a successor to hand the mantle to, there is no success. Now that PDM has a network in place for raising up spiritual sons and daughters we rarely use the "Elisha" style of ministry development. For those who do not have a network and are seasoned enough to train others in prophetic ministry I hope you will consider the above as one option for building and releasing new prophets into the Church.

The Dark Side Of Prophecy

I wanted to take a moment to talk about something no one has been comfortable addressing. It is what I call the "dark side" of prophecy, and young prophets need to be made aware of it. What I mean is, prophets and their words can be used in the wrong way, and they may be caught in the crossfire between leadership and congregation members. There are occasions when wrong teaching, fear or even manipulation can push leadership into using a valid prophetic word to control a difficult, or unresolved situation. I have seen this happen to good people in both the market place and in the church, and it never turns out well. In developing young prophets I like to be sure they really understand exactly what this is all about.

In this scenario, there is usually a disagreement that has happened in ideology, and the one in leadership feels one of the tools at their disposal is the prophetic word a prophet spoke over the other person. The word is brought out, and selected portions of it are used to convince the individual that their thinking or decision is wrong. Worse yet, the leader may present the idea that the person is out of "God's will", and unless they comply, they will live a second-class life or have a tragically unfulfilled ministry. At times like this, leaders will call prophets to support their position in using the prophetic word they delivered. It is usually not in the best interest of any prophet to let themselves be drawn into such church activity.

In some rare cases bad decisions might actually be "rebellion" that needs to be addressed by a leader. However, 99% of the time there has been nothing more than poor communication, or a simple disagreement that has happened. This is never to be misconstrued with defiance to authority. However, when a prophetic word is brought up, it tends to shake most Christians right to the core. Typically using this trump card is based in ignorance of the word or fear. It may also be wrong teaching or a last resort attempt to control those who are in an unhealthy church. Some of the wrong teaching I myself have had to repent of. As I matured in my calling, I realized that the beliefs held by those who were prophetic pioneers, were not always built on solid biblical ground. Below is a case in point.

I, and many other prophets, taught an "all or not at all" concept of prophecy for years. That is, we believed that prophetic words were tied to the place where they were spoken. That was especially thought to be true if it came in a prophetic presbytery meeting. Yet the Bible says *"... the gifts and calling of God are without repentance"* (Roman 11:29). This means what you are called to do does not go away, or become negated, because you may have changed your church. God gave you that calling, and it will stand firm in your life. When God gave me a clearer understanding of this, I soon realized that prophecy is not necessarily place specific. However, according to Scripture it is always heart specific. Prophecy unfolds due to the condition of your heart, and your desire to serve God. It is not so much a result of the physical location of your body.

Location is important, but it is not all there is when it comes to people being in "God's will." We have had people leave our church and they are now walking in what was prophesied over them when they were with us. David's call to be king was valid when he was in Jerusalem and it was still valid when he was running for his life in the wilderness. God uses all things for the good for those that love Him and are called according to

His purposes. This is Romans 8:28, and it means exactly what it says. If you keep a good heart, you can still move forward by the grace of God, into your calling even if you must go elsewhere.

This is a powerfully liberating revelation that needs to be understood and embraced. When a valid prophetic word is spoken over your life, the content of that word has more meaning than the location of where it was spoken. Unless a prophet says specifically that you must stay in "this" specific place, you are not necessarily out of God's will if you leave. More importantly, the ministries you have are not bound up in one place, even though they may have been designed to benefit that place.

It is true that words spoken in prophetic presbytery are released to church members with the intent that they will be worked out in that particular church. This is why you have prophetic presbytery. It identifies who is called to do what in that church. The person and the place are definitely linked together through that word. As they stay faithful in that congregation, the word will come to pass. There is a spiritual reality and a natural connection that should be honored. Even with that, there is a much higher and bigger picture in God's mind for how your ministry can find its full expression.

The picture in God's mind is always higher and bigger than just one moment or one location.

Consider this: if something happens and your church closes, does that mean all those who went there, and got prophetic words for that place, will never fulfill their ministry? Of course not! We all know the people of the church would go elsewhere to fulfill their ministry. In the same way, if you do not remain in the place you got a particular word, it does not mean you have thrown your life, or your ministry away. God is not that narrow in anything He does. Your ministry is still your ministry, but it will find its expression in some other place of service. No one's ministry ends up on the trash heap just because they changed churches. The only thing that changes is where your ministry will now be fulfilled. Your responsibility is to make sure your heart remains tender, you stay teachable, and you remain faithful in the new congregation you have joined.

What about the big "GW"—God's Will? If I leave the church that was "God's Will" for my life, what then? What about that one and only place I have to be, or I have missed God? Well, it's just like those who marry and then divorce. This is certainly not God's will, but it still happens, and it's not the end of the world. When a marriage is totally unworkable, unsafe, abusive, or when the covenant has been violated, a divorce is going to happen. In order to keep the one who is in danger safe, the union ends. It is exactly the same way in a local church.

Please don't misunderstand what I just said. I believe God does have a church for each of us, but He also gives us the freedom to find a new church if things become unhealthy or traumatic where we are. If we can no longer receive in that place, if there is a long, painful unresolved history that is killing us, it is then time to find a safer place to go. That does not mean we can church hop, and just run off every time things get uncomfortable. No, we need to be a people of loyalty and commitment, just like David. Yet even David knew, when things got deadly he had to leave. If things become unfit for you, and you feel like you and your family are dying in your church, then it is your responsibility to stay alive by finding another shepherd, and joining another sheepfold.

I have seen the dark side of prophecy pop up when pastors used it to whip someone into shape, or hold on to them when it really was appropriate for them to leave. Out came all the prophetic words the person ever got, from any source that gave it. Aunt Tilly's word, the prayer group, a one-time preacher who spoke at church, dreams from years past and feelings others had are all pulled out. These are pieced together, and placed on equal ground to be cited as proof that things must go a certain way. They become shackles to keep the person bound to a location, or forced into a ministry they simply don't feel called to.

Insecure pastors, or those who have very small congregations often, want to hold on to the few people they have. That's because once a certain declining number is reached, it is impossible to run the ministries of a church. Without realizing it, fear of people leaving can bring with it a spirit of control to keep them there. This attempt to hold people in place brings guilt or questions personal loyalty, and both of these are deadly.

Unfortunately, prophetic words are easily used for this purpose and it causes the dark side of prophecy to manifest. When you see such things beginning to happen, my suggestion is to graciously walk away, and don't look back. Don't criticize, argue, defend your decision or let yourself become resentful and bitter. Just move on and find a new church that will help you heal up. Here you can get the encouragement you need to move into what God has called you to do.

A Market Place Example

I know of an instance where prophecy was nearly used incorrectly in the market place a number of years back. A church leader, who was also a businessman, had received a prophetic word about mentoring some of the young men in his church. He was to develop them in basic sound business principles and help them get an ethical and biblical foundation in their business life.

Unfortunately his interpretation of that word was very different from its intended purpose. He immediately started bring all these prime young men into his own business in order to build it up. Needless to say, his pastor did not see things the same way, and a very difficult conflict erupted. This unhealthy diversion soon caused a division that had to be addressed. After the pastor met with this man, it was clear money was at the core of the problem and he was not going to accept biblical correction.

Not long after this, the business overseer of this man was informed of the resistance that had happened. He knew it would prevent what could be financial increase for both of them. Thus, he took the prophetic word, without saying anything to the pastor and set up a meeting with the pastor's overseeing apostle. In that meeting the man attempted to use the prophetic word to usurp the pastor's authority. Needless to say the apostle saw things for what they were, and the meeting did not conclude as the businessmen had hoped.

In the end the church maintained its integrity and the pastor was able to head off the conflict. Unfortunately the businessman was unwilling to submit under pastoral authority. He eventually left the church and failed to fulfill his prophetic potential in that place. In leaving as he did, he not only hurt himself, but he also hindered God's design for that church. The young men never got the mentoring God intended and sadly, everyone was negatively impacted. Worst of all, the enemy was the only one left rejoicing when everything finally concluded.

None of the above were bad people, but each had their own idea of what they thought the prophetic word was to be used for. The point being made is that prophecy can fall from its intended biblical purpose to bless and build people up. In the wrong hands, a prophetic word can be used to bring about a dark, unintended results, and this needs to be guarded against. Young prophets must learn to recognize this and refuse to participate in it. No doubt this kind of thing grieves the heart of God because it wounds the people involved, and hurts the spiritual life of the local church. In addition, it gives prophecy a bad name and brings the ministry of every genuine prophet into question. As young prophets learn how to identify and expose this illegitimate use of prophecy, they will secure the integrity of their own ministry, and preserve the honor of the prophetic office.

Identifying Genuine Prophets

In closing this chapter I wanted to lay a foundation for young prophets and church leaders, on how to clearly identify a genuine prophet from those who simply operate in the gifts. In my mind, most of the confusion seems to come from a lack of teaching, and even more so from the misuse of the word "prophetic." That is, every activity of the Holy Spirit now seems to have the word "prophetic" attached to it, and that has created most of the problem.

For instance, we have heard the term "prophetic worship" thrown about since the early 1970s and yet scripturally speaking only prophets can produce genuine prophetic worship. We see a clear example of this in 1 Samuel 10:5-6. Saul encounters this group of prophet/musicians coming down off the mountain, and it changed the future king into another man.

The best worship is always Spirit led, but that does not mean it is biblically correct to call it prophetic worship. The same goes for prayer. Why is Spirit led pray now called prophetic intercession? Are all those praying now prophets? David certainly is a great example of one who did do prophetic intercession, and the Book of Psalms is proof of that. However, let's not be misinformed by saying that Spirit led prayer is now "prophetic" because it's not. Effective prayer is simply Spirit led and let's leave it at that!

Then there is the whole misguided concept of "prophetic dreams." No, these are simply Spirit led dreams which confirm God's word that says, *"He gives to his beloved even in his sleep"* (Ps. 127:2 NASB). When people call Spirit led dreams "prophetic dreams" it is simply incorrect theology.

Spirit led dreams are one way that God speaks to people. Often they are another aspect of the word of knowledge, perhaps the word of wisdom or even the gift of prophecy. They are not necessarily "prophetic" and you don't have to be a prophet to have one. In fact Pharaoh did have a genuine "prophetic dream" and Joseph was able to interpret it to save the whole nation. That being said, Pharaoh was not a prophet and we should not call a Spirit led dream a "prophetic" dream unless it really is.

Finally we have the concept of "prophetic conferences." I have attended and taught at many of these over the years, and for the most part they were not prophetic at all. I would say that 98% of those who attended were not prophets and there was very little prophetic revelation released. What went on there was basic teaching about the power of gifts, spirit led worship, gift activation and the experimental use of the gifts. Let me state once again that none of this is prophetic. Thus, when we call this a "prophetic conference," it simply is not true and it adds to the over all confusion of the church.

Characteristics of Genuine Prophets

Now that I have cleared away some of the spiritual fog, lets look a bit deeper at how to recognize prophets. Genuine prophets have specific earmarks that tell you who they are. What follows is a basic overview of those identifying characteristics.

1. **Genuine prophets do not need to filter what they receive from God through the gifts, or through natural feelings, promptings or awarenesses.** Prophets can simply open their mouths and speak according to Ps. 81:10. *"... open your mouth and I will fill it ..."* In addition Ps. 42:7 says *"... deep calls unto deep ..."* That is, the deep things of God connect to and resonate with the deep things of the Spirit within every prophet. Prophets speak from that direct "deep-to-deep" connection because of

the ministry they have, and the spiritual design within them from God.

2. **Genuine prophets have the secret counsel of God revealed to them according to Amos 3:7.** They know what God is doing and can speak it with clarity when He tells them to. They are not in confusion but have specific clarity when others don't.

3. **Genuine prophets speak to the future.** Acts 11:27 and Acts 21:10 are clear examples of this. The prophet Agabus reveals the future with clarity and accuracy, and that was the confirming proof of his ministry as a prophet. David did the same throughout the Book of Psalms as did other prophets in Scripture.

4. **Genuine prophets here God's voice directly and they have direct profound encounters with God.** Exodus 4:4 identifies the encounter Moses had with God when he was called to that ministry. Look at Daniel, Ezekiel and John for other examples of this.

5. **Genuine prophets speak with insight and authority.** They identify the things of God to their generation to provide guidance. They speak, teach and minister with a revelatory edge that others do not have. They don't just warm up the teachings of others, they get fresh insight from the secret place of God and unlock the mysteries of the word in a new and unique ways. In Exodus 19:1-7 Moses demonstrates this and in Luke 2:37 the prophetess Anna does the same, as does John the Revelator.

6. **Genuine prophets will have the past revealed to them in profound and unique ways.** God does this with them in order to bring insight about it for the present and vision for the future. Moses wrote the book of Genesis as a revelation of the past so that the nation of Israel would have a foundation for their present and insight for their future. The writer of Proverbs 8:23-31 give another powerful example of this very thing.

7. **Genuine prophets carry an anointing that impacts those who get near them.** This anointing can cause others to do what they normally could not. 1 Samuel 10:5-6 is a beautiful example of this when Saul begins to prophesy. Again in 1 Samuel 19:20-24 we see this same thing happen. Numbers 11:25 shows the same process. God took of the Spirit that was on Moses and placed it on the seventy so they all prophesied, but they never did it again. When prophets come into a church a deposit is often left that stirs the atmosphere and brings the spiritual activity up in the church.

8. **Genuine prophets speak with specificity and authority into the lives of the people and nations God has sent them to.** They do not act independently of the design of God. They live a life of obedience and loyalty to the authority God has called them to serve, even if their message is not well received. Examine the lives of Joseph, Daniel, Elijah, Isaiah, John the Baptist and others and you will see these principles in full bloom.

Every genuine prophet I know has had experiences with the above at one time or another. This is what identifies them as the real thing. It sets them apart from those who simply have well developed gifts. Those who operate in the gifts may learn to use them in unique ways over time. Some may demonstrate profound abilities, but flowing in well-developed gifts does make someone a prophet.

Being a prophet is a call of God not a learned skill. Those who are prophets were not taught it at a conference; they did not learn it from a book or become a prophet by taking a college class. They received it from the Lord and are waking it out through a lifetime of deep relationship with Him, study of the Word, worship and obedience to His will.

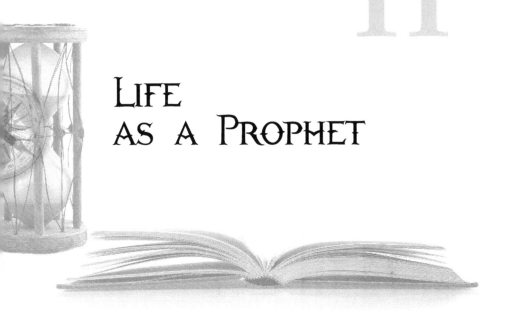

LIFE AS A PROPHET

Over the years, I have been asked on numerous occasions how I do what I do. How exactly do I get what I get from God? The answer to that question is never simple. What I do know is this, as my life and relationship with the Lord has developed, the ministry has also developed, and the way He spoke to me developed as well. Scripture instructs to draw near to God and He will draw near to you. Your responsibility is to discover how to get close to Him and stay there. That positions you correctly to hear His voice, know His heart and receive revelation from the Holy Spirit.

When I first became aware of my calling as a prophet most of my prophetic ministry revolved around spontaneous songs. God gave me these while I was leading worship or just playing my guitar. I would instantly get a song or a few lines of a song for a certain individual, or a specific occasion. These might be detailed prophecies I sang over someone in a service or something that came when people asked me to write a song for their wedding. Through this I gained a reputation as a prophetic psalmist and this opened the door for me to do worship seminars and lead worship in different meetings and regional conferences.

As time went on I learned that I did not need to be singing or worshiping to step into the Spirit. God broke open an entirely new realm to me one day as I was standing in front of someone. I actually saw a river flowing before me from left to right and I knew it was the river of their life. The future for them was to my left, their present was directly in front of me and their past was to my right.

When I first realized what this was, and knew that God was showing me the person's entire life, I just jumped right into the stream. I was immediately overwhelmed and then gripped by a flood of emotions, feelings, visions, revelation and information that swirled around me. It felt like I was being swept away by a rapidly moving flash flood and I was about to drown in sensory overload. Needless to say I knew I was way in over my head but I had caught a glimpse of all that was available in the Spirit.

The next time I saw this river and jumped in I felt God's hand pick me up and put me back on the riverbank. He then instructed me to "throw a bucket in the river" and look at what was inside the bucket when I pulled it out. Within would be all the revelation I could handle at that moment. I learned that when I threw it up stream, or to my left, I could look into someone's future. If I threw the bucket directly in front of me I could see pieces of their present, and if I threw it to my right, or downstream, I could see glimpses of their past. This was simple, clear and it worked well for a number of years.

During this same time a battle began within me that I had never experienced before. Every time I was waiting to release a prophetic word, especially during prophetic presbytery, I would hear a mocking voice. It came with great deception to taunt me and bring fear. It would say things like, "Who do you think you are? You have just been lucky up to this point. Sooner or later people will find out that you are a fraud. You are not a prophet, you're a joke! You're nothing, and you know you have nothing to say. You are a back-woods hick and a failure who is way out of his league. You've got nothing. You know you're just making it all up and that means you are a liar as well! Stop doing this before you humiliate and embarrass yourself, and people find out the truth."

When this voice came I would be paralyzed with fear and began to doubt everything I had done and experienced in God. I would sit there terrified to open my mouth because I worried that God would rebuke me for being a false prophet and a liar. I prayed, I cried out to God and repented of everything I could think of. Then I would press beyond all the emotions and force myself to step out and prophesy anyway. It was a running battle that I silently endured every time I was doing any kind of prophetic ministry.

Paralyzing fear caused me to doubt everything I had experienced in God.

This internal war went on for a long time and I was too ashamed to tell anyone what was happening. Then one day it finally dawned on me who was doing the talking. I realized that a demon had been assigned to me and his job was to attack, torment and distract me from the very thing I was called to do. With this revelation I bound up that demonic tormenting, lying spirit every time it spoke. After I had gotten a few solid victories in the battlefield of my mind and emotions, the war was over. Not long afterwards the accusing voice basically faded into the distance and I was free of it.

With this change, God began to speak to me in what looked like black and white or color pictures, and at other times in what looked like video clips. I would see these things like panoramic movies playing before me in the spirit. At other times I would feel emotions, get an image, feel a sensation, smell something or have a thought or a single word just pass through my mind for no reason. Even the other gifts began to take on new and wonderful expressions. An example of this began to happen with the gift of tongues.

My wife and I were in in Thetford Mines, Quebec doing a series of meetings and a Canadian Apostle named Dennie Bienvenue asked to meet with us. He was friends with our host pastors and wanted to check us out to see what was really in our hearts. The pastors invited him to join us for a time of prayer so we got together one evening. As we began praying in the spirit I started speaking in what sounded like a dialect of French. I had done it before so for me it was no surprise. However, at this point Dennie began to laugh and said "This prophet is prophesying and doesn't even know what he is saying. I understand every word you are speaking."

Apparently he had done ministry among the Inuit Indians in northern Hudson Bay and knew their language. He had been among them when a revival broken out several years before and knew they called the Holy Spirit the "Blue Wind." He said I was speaking their language, called "First Nation," which is a mixture of old French and the old Inuit language. He went on to explain that I had been prophesying about the Blue Wind of the North coming to the northern area of Canada and Quebec, and how it would sweep down into the south and spark a fresh revival in eastern Canada and the US."

On another occasion I was in an international airport and had just gotten the news my flight was delayed. Frankly, I was bored, and that is not a good thing because I always find a way to entertain myself. I decided to pray in tongues but I would do it with a twist. I would speak into my phone as if I was having a conversation with someone but speak in tongues. As I walked around I would get up alongside those speaking in another language and God would just give me that language as I began to speak. Time and time again the people would look at me and smile. Some even nodded while others had a look of shock on their faces. I had no idea what I was saying but apparently they did. Now I am looking for ways to follow up with this unique operation of tongues and lead people to Christ.

Over time things of the Spirit became more and more real. I would see colored objects that had symbolic or literal meanings for those I prophesied to. I would see scripture, or even see a word superimposed on someone, or in the space around them. I might see something imprinted on the bottom of a shoe, on a book cover or even a billboard. I also began to audibly hear specific words or phrases spoken by a rich, deep masculine voice. A few times I was caught up in the spirit and saw things in heaven as I was prophesying over those God pointed out to me.

One unique thing that never happened to me up to that point, was prophetic dreams. Scripture says that God gives to His beloved even in his sleep, so I wanted that experience. My wife has always been an avid prophetic dreamer, so one day I asked her to lay hands on me and pray for an impartation. From that point on the dreams started and they have never stopped. I actually keep a notebook by my bedside to record each one and they have been a great blessing on numerous occasions.

One instance of this was the first time I dreamed about tornadoes. There were three of them that tore by our church building. They brought massive destruction all around them but were unable to bring the building down. When I awoke I wrote it down but had no idea what it represented. Within a month, three people in our congregation went on a rampage and began to verbally attack my wife, our leadership team, and me. Eventually they departed in anger, but the church was basically left unharmed.

From that experience I learned every time I dream about tornadoes the number of them corresponds to the number of people we are going to have to deal with. It never fails! However, there are other symbols that God has given me as well, and over time I have learned what each means. It is just another way the Holy Spirit can communicate the things of the Kingdom and we should all be open to enjoying that avenue of spiritual expression.

In time I came to a place where God began to open the Spirit realm to me in the form of a portal. This opening would be high above me in heaven, directly over my head. It looked like a doorway filled with liquid, gold light. I would see or sense a shaft of light flowing from this opening and knew it went directly into my head and spirit. When it came I could relax in the spirit and poke my head up through that portal to look into the heavenly realm. In that place all I did as a prophet, and all I needed for ministry, was found with ease. It was simple and available to me any time the portal was there.

Finally I came to a place where God really set my ministry free. He showed me that as a prophet, if I would **God told me to just open my mouth and speak.** stay in relationship with Him, and remain obedient to Him, He no longer needed to prime my prophetic pump with visions, words, images or feelings. I was a prophet that He recognized, and because of that He would always back me up. All I had to do was trust Him at a new level. He then gave me Psalm 81:10 which says:

"I, the LORD, am your God, Who brought you up from the land of Egypt; Open your mouth wide and I will fill it."

The night this happened I ended up being the lead prophet in a prophetic presbytery meeting at a large church in Rochester, New York. Three of us were there to do several prophetic presbytery meetings. When the first couple sat down I was just pushed forward. As I walked towards them I had no feelings, no images, no helps, hints, no visions or clear words. I had nothing at all, and I was nearly in a panic wondering why.

I immediately heard that mocking voice again and had to fight back a wave of anxiety that washed over me. God had decided this was the night He would thrust me into that new level as a prophet and He did it when it was impossible for me to back out. With all this going on inside me, I walked across the platform knowing I had nothing to say. I felt alone, totally helpless and absolutely empty. Once I silenced that mocking voice I just stood there not knowing what to do. It was then that I heard the voice of the Lord say "open your mouth and I will fill it."

Out of shear desperation I did just that. I literally opened my mouth without a clue about what I would say, and started to make a noise. What amazed me was at the moment I spoke that first syllable, it turned into a word that got connected to a sentence. The sentence produced a paragraph, which was followed by another and then another. This ended up bringing forth a magnificent, clear prophecy that deeply touched the couple sitting in front of me on many levels.

All of this happened very quickly but I realized when it was over that God had indeed brought me to a new place as a prophet. That night He showed me how I could trust Him to let a pure word from Him come right out of my spirit. It bypassed my thoughts and missed my emotions all together. It was simple, elegant, powerful, accurate, clear and full of God's truth, grace and life. The impact this had on me, and my perception of prophecy, was astounding. I felt like I had been released from a prison and was free to flow in a totally new way with the Holy Spirit.

What I came to realize was that the highest level of prophetic ministry always flows directly from God's Spirit, and out through my spirit. The

Bible says this is where "deep calls unto deep." As a prophet there is no need for me to have physical promptings, emotional hooks or something highlighted in the natural to make me aware of what God wants to say. Not that these things are wrong. For many years, I have taught people how to hear God this way. However, for a prophet this is a lower operation of things and automatically imposes a limiting factor. When I am dependent on cues from natural phenomena to release a spiritual reality, I have tied the things of the Spirit to this earthly realm. Please make note that even though it works, this is the reverse of how prophets are called to release the Kingdom.

As a prophet, I began to understand that staying in a state of readiness meant God could simply flow right through me at any moment to unveil His Kingdom. I did not need to feel, see, smell, taste or hear anything first. These natural promptings are basically used to get our attention because we are so anchored in the natural world. Think about it for one second. Scripture says clearly that the natural man does not understand the things of the Sprit. If that is true, then running everything through a natural filter first is certainly not the best way for prophets to release their ministry.

Remember, just as God is three and yet one, we are also created in that same image. We are body, soul and spirit. Our natural body is designed by God to be aware of the surroundings we are in. It is conscious of the environment and it connects us to the natural world around us. Our soul is designed by God to be conscious of our emotional and intellectual environment. Through this we are self-conscious. However, it is our spirit that is in direct contact with the Holy Spirit. Through this we are God-conscious and His Kingdom is revealed, understood and released.

I finally understood that prophets are very different from those who simply flow in the gifts. They are specifically designed by God to operate from a pure, spiritual perspective. They don't need natural cues, hints or promptings for the Kingdom to be released through them. God created them to be unconscious to the natural but open for the supernatural. It is this life calling to live in the spirit, and be a willing, unconscious conduit for God, that gives them such a unique place in God's creation.

A second instance of this happened not long afterward when I stopped to eat lunch with prophets James Berkley, Timothy Sherman, Apostle Rick Menard and a few other ministers. We were in New Hampshire at some meetings and decided to get something to eat. We were talking about "power evangelism" with those who had joined us, as we waited to order. I had just finished a mini sermon on how the gifts were a great way to bring people to Christ, and how Jesus used them in the Gospels, when our waitress came to the table.

She began to ask me what I wanted, and I opened my mouth to say, "I would like a hamburger." However, what came out was not that at all. I heard myself speaking to the young waitress that she had just purchased two airline tickets, and that she was getting ready to fly back to Malaysia. She was taking the trip to see her family, whom she had not seen in a very long time. When I finished the girl was frozen in midsentence and stood there staring at me with wide-open eyes.

Everyone at the table, myself included, sat there smiling at what had just happened. There was a moment of stunned quiet and then I looked right at her to see the reaction. She stood there clutching her tray and tears began to stream down her face. She said, "How could you possibly know that? It's true, what you said is all true, all of it."

I explained that God loved her and had made Himself real to her so she could give her heart and life to Him. In the next 30 seconds she and I prayed together. I led this young woman to the Lord right there in the restaurant as everyone was looking on. God had given the whole group a first-hand experience of power evangelism just because I opened my mouth. What He was telling us at that moment was simple. This is actually available to anyone if they would just learn to trust Him. That was a whole new realm of the prophetic I had never experienced, or expected, and it was wonderful.

From that point until this present day I never know exactly what God might want to do with me. I have remained open and flexible so that I don't miss any of the adventures He wants to take me on. Several times I have been caught up into heaven and seen the departed loved ones of people I'm ministering to. I once saw a woman standing in heaven as I called her husband of 46 years forward to receive ministry. God had let me see the man in a vision the night before. In that vision he was standing at the back of the church all alone leaning against the wall and I knew he would be in this meeting. So, the next day when I saw him standing in that exact place I asked him to come forward. As he walked up to the front of the church I saw the woman mentioned above.

What I did not know was that this woman was his wife who had died three months earlier. He was broken hearted and despondent with grief. He just needed to know his sweetheart was with Jesus. What no one knew was that in his heart he had decided that God might not be real, and this was going to be his last church meeting. However, the Holy Spirit used me to provide the comfort and confirmation he so desperately had to have. When I shared what I was seeing the man began to wipe tears from his eyes. As far as I know he is still in church just because I was used to show the amazing compassion of a loving God. All I had to be was a willing vessel and it's the same with you.

All you have to do is be a willing vessel.

Another lesson I had to learn about moving in the Spirit happened in 2001. Lance Wallnau, Rita Fedele and I were doing a prophetic conference together that spring, and at the end of the meetings Lance asked Rita and I to prophesy over him. I quickly handed Rita the microphone and she delivered a wonderfully clear, well-formed word. It was clean, rhythmic and flowed out with great ease and power.

Then Rita handed the microphone back to me and I realized I was struggling. God had only given me two simple things to say. As I compared that with what she had just delivered I felt almost embarrassed. In all honesty the thought crossed my mind, "Why even bother?" Yet that was all I had, so I forced myself to speak something like the following over Lance. "God is going to open a door for you to stand before an international governing body. When you do, use wisdom to share the truths of the Kingdom and you will have a second opportunity as well." Once that was said I stepped back, looked at it from a natural perspective and a war went on inside me. I really wanted to apologize to these mighty ministers of God for my poor performance.

Years went by and all of us went on with our ministries. Then one day I had a brief encounter with Lance and as we spoke God brought that word back to my mind when Lance told me he had been given an opportunity to address the United Nations. He actually had shared biblical principles with that international governing body. However, he had made a mistake and was not sure if he would get a second invitation. Apparently he went in there with guns blazing instead of using wisdom by acting more like a stealth bomber to deliver his powerful message.

The moment he said the above I realized just how significant that simple prophetic word had been which I had delivered to him years earlier. More importantly, I realized there are no insignificant words from God. The length of a word God gives a prophet to speak is never to be questioned. That is not what makes it valuable, or full of power. Speaking exactly what God wants spoken is what really matters. Never forget that point! The moment a prophet begins to make comparisons about what is being delivered, they will be ruled by natural thinking and their ministry is basically over.

Life Is An Adventure

As a prophet I have to embrace the fact that life with God is an adventure. There are constant changes and continual challenges that I am presented with and must adjust to. Some things have rocked my world while others have not yet come to pass. A dear friend of mine, prophet James Berkley, presented one such radical thing to me. James and I met years ago when we were both doing ministry in New England. After he watched me leading worship and doing prophetic ministry, he brought me into one of his more unique ideas.

James wanted to take a team of seasoned prophets into the culture of Hollywood to minister the Word of the Lord to those in the entertainment industry. His concept was to go in first with a team of intercessors to disrupt the demonic atmosphere and open up heaven. Then he, and I, Timothy Sherman and several other prophets he trusted would set up a time to prophesy on television, to those he knew in the movie industry.

His vision was to first teach the people in Hollywood from God's Word about prophetic ministry. Next he wanted to openly challenge and expose people to the truth by demonstrating the Kingdom of God through genuine prophets. By doing this he believed it would dethrone the demonic influence of psychics in that industry. James was upset that these false prophets had free access into the movie business for years. He believed that seasoned prophets of God should be the ones in that mountain of influence.

He had a vision to invade Hollywood with true men and women of God and by so doing release the power of the Holy Spirit into the culture. However, before the plan could ever be put in place something happened. James finished ministering a great service one day and then sat down on the platform. As he quietly waited for the service to conclude the expression on his face changed and he simply fell over and died on the spot. He slipped right over into Glory. Who knows, his vision may yet come to pass.

Prophecy Made A Difference

The powerful change that prophetic ministry can make was made evident to me once again a few years back. My wife, and I and Apostle Rick Callahan were doing prophetic presbytery in Albany, NY. During that meeting one young couple was brought forward and seated before the church to receive ministry. The moment I placed my hands on them I was pulled into the Spirit and back in time about one hour.

I found myself in the back seat of a car that was traveling on a local highway. I could feel the vibration of the road as I looked out the window at all the traffic that was passing by. In the front seat sat this same couple and I knew they were on their way to the meeting we were actually doing. As we road along the two were having a deep conversation. I saw the husband turn to his wife and say, "All I know is they better have something pretty specific to tell me if I am going to believe all this prophecy stuff." The wife listened, made a few comments and reassured him that they only needed to relax and see what would happen.

As I began to explain all the details of what I was experiencing the couple looked at each other in total amazement. They both knew this was indeed the exact conversation they had with each other on their way to that meeting. I was actually repeating back to the husband, word for word, what he had said to his wife in the privacy of their own car. The point is, God heard the cry of his heart and allowed me to ride along with them for that moment in time in order to confirm to him that prophecy, and prophets, are the real deal.

The end result was that they received the ministry and had a life-changing experience because God met them where they were at. This is one of the biggest benefits that genuine prophets bring with them. When prophetic ministry is applied correctly it changes lives and removes fears. It brings healing, provides direction and may also bring correction, but it is all done in love. Prophecy can do in a few moments what it might take a counselor month or even years to accomplish. When God makes Himself real through the voice of a prophet, heaven invades earth and life is never the same.

Basic Principles

The reality for living life as a prophet has some basic principles that continually flow through it. The first is that you must stay hungry and you must stay close to the Lord. He is the source of all that you will ever do. If you wander from His side, or the voice of the Holy Spirit, you are done. The second is that you must be willing to take risks and try things that seem impossible. In addition you must be comfortable with making mistakes and looking like a fool from time to time. Last of all you must be willing to not let the criticism and unbelief of others discourage you from your calling. If you embrace and enjoy living this way than chances are you really do have what it takes to be a New Testament prophet.

Prophets, prophecy and the prophetic realm are not some mysterious, highly secret place in God. Prophets are not some set-apart, elect group who lord it over others. They are simply men and women who know their calling and gifts. They have chosen a lifestyle that draws them close to God and they are willing to be His ambassadors to a lost and broken world. Most of all, they know that humility and relationship with God is what keeps their ministry pure and acceptable to Him.

Anyone can walk with power and revelation according to the design of God for their life. What He has placed in you is unique and needs to be developed, nurtured and treasured. Embrace, study and feast upon His Word and seek His will. As you do, you will come to better understand the things He has freely given to you. With that knowledge in hand you will be equipped to face the challenges of every new day and soar into the high places of the Spirit.

If you are called as a prophet, then you should stay humble and continue to press into the full sphere of authority you have been given. Others are depending on you to find your place in God, so you can help them find theirs. If you are not called as a prophet but do operate in one or more of the other levels of the prophetic, be encouraged to keep seeking His face. With joy, become the prophetic person God designed you to be.

I was told the following many years ago by another prophet who is a friend of mine. He said, "Bill, failure has nothing to do with making a mistake. Failure only happens when you quit trying. You're a good prophet and you'll get better because I know you'll never stop trying." When it comes to the prophetic realm, do not let failure or intimidation be an option for you. Try, try and try again! Accept and learn to love correction. Hunger after God, stay humble and never promote yourself. These simple keys unlock every ministry and they will unlock you!

Failure only happens when you quit trying. Never give up.

I encourage you to get beside those who know more than you. Ask questions and learn from their ministry. Study the Word and pray in tongues. If you can, "shadow" mature ministry for a season and watch what they do from a place on the sidelines. Let their prophetic mantle mix with yours and watch for the combined anointing that results. You will be amazed at how much of who they are can rub off on you. Not that you want to be a copy of someone else, but you want the best of what they have to be sown as seed into what God has called you to do.

Listen to the teaching of other prophets and learn their heart so you can follow their example. Embrace correction and above all don't strive for "your ministry." Ministry is the final outcome of all who walk in the principles outlined above. The thing is, you never have to seek ministry because God is the One who gives it freely. My experience has been that those who do these things will not be disappointed.

Final Thoughts

I have had many profound experiences since 1976 and I am believing God for many more. I am looking for dramatic healings, miracles that rock nations and times of physically being transported to new locations by the spirit. I want a much deeper revelation of Scripture that brings new light and liberty. I want to deliver dynamic personal prophecies to world leaders, and life changing words to all who need it. I want to be one of those God trusts to shake the kingdom of darkness and break the power of the enemy every place I go.

Most of all I want a deeper, more intimate relationship with the Lord. He is my wellspring of life and one great passion. Through intimate relationship with Him will come magnificent, unexplainable encounters in the Spirit, and new prophetic songs. Through Him will come things that shake me to the core, leave me breathless and make me hungry for more. I want an overabundance of finances to bless others and build the Kingdom of God. I guess you could say I am open to every Kingdom reality that is available. Simply put, I want it all, and I know God wants to give it to me if I will only believe and do what He says!

No doubt other prophets have had their own journey with God, and hear Him in their own way. The fact is, there is no simple formula and no right or wrong way to hear God. This is just how He has dealt with me. The point in sharing all of this is to show you that the ability and experiences any prophet has will always be developed through a life-long walk of love and faith. We are all a work in progress and our ability to hear God continues to unfold from year to year, so we can continue to bless His people.

God is the One who lifts one ministry up and sets another down. Let Him teach you by His Spirit what you need to know, where you need to go and how you need to change. Let him bring you the divine alignments and personal connections that hold your destiny and unlock your ministry. Only He can bring you to the people, places and truths that will allow you to be successful in His eyes.

The thing is, when it comes to establishing a successful ministry, you will have to embrace the fact that you are going to make mistakes. There is no way to avoid it. You also have to keep in mind that these will either be used by the enemy to discourage and define you, or you can let the Holy Spirit use them to teach and refine you. The choice is up to you! Once you get that settled in your heart you are on your way to becoming the prophetic person God has made you to be.

My final prayer is that this book may be one of many tools God uses to help you on your journey. May it make your pathway clear, rich and full of His spiritual substance. May the concepts and precepts presented here shape your ideas, adjust your vision and compel you forward on this grand adventure of prophets, prophecy and life in the Holy Spirit.

. . . .

Only God can
bring you to the
people, places
and truths that
will allow you
to be successful
in His eyes.

. . . .

THE MINISTRY OF PDM

Prophetic Destiny Ministry is dedicated to the purpose of bringing the Body of Christ to full maturity. Bill and Esther Emmons are strong, seasoned apostolic prophets, teachers, lovers of prayer and true worshipers of God. They desire to see the Saints established in the faith, passionately in love with Jesus, radically expressive in worship and hungry to move with purity in demonstrating things of the Kingdom.

Bill and Esther have also started the PDM network through which they hope to provide spiritual covering, training and connections for five-fold ministers with the added focus of identifying and developing those who are called to prophetic ministry. The vision of the PDM network is to re-establish an Ephesians 2:20 model of apostolic and prophetic teamwork that builds the foundations of the local church as God intended. If you are interested in more information about the PDM network please go to our website, www.pdministry.org and click on the "PDM network" link.

Bill and Esther are available throughout the year to teach, preach and minister prophetically in local churches, leadership meetings, conferences, and doing prophetic presbytery with the laying on of hands. For more information on PDM, or to find our schedule for booking meetings, please go to our website at www.pdministry.org. You may also email us at or wemmons@gmail.com.

· · · · · · · · · · · ·

www.pdministry.org

· · · · · · · · · · · ·

Made in the USA
Middletown, DE
16 February 2023

25043114R00124